SCIENCE FOR PARENTS

COPYRIGHT © 2015 BY KARLA TALANIAN

All rights reserved.

ISBN-13:   978-1500598143

ISBN-10:   1500598143

Available from Amazon.com, CreateSpace.com, and other retail outlets

Cover design by Karissa Talanian

Cover photo courtesy of NASA's Goddard Space Flight Center. Data from two missions, NASA's Lunar Reconnaissance Orbiter its Gravity Recovery and Interior Laboratory (GRAIL) have been combined to examine the lunar body tide, that is, the effect that the Earth's gravity has on the moon. The moon also exerts a gravitational pull on the earth, but here it is our oceans that react most noticeable. Since the moon is dry, the Earth's gravitational pull results in a small (about 20 inches, or 51cm) but distinct deformation in the solid lunar body itself.

Back Cover photo courtesy of NASA/JSC Gateway to Astronaut Photography of Earth.
This photo was taken by astronauts in the International Space Station in July, 2011. The colors illustrate the different chemical compositions of the different layers of the Earth's atmosphere. The troposphere shows up in bright orange.

Science
for Parents

... And also for grandparents, nannies, much admired big brothers and sisters, really cool aunts and uncles, etc.

Curiosity about nature is the beginning of understanding science

Have you ever stared at a page of your kid's science homework, and just shrugged? This book will turn your frustration into a beautiful "Ah-Ha" moment for both of you to share. It will enable you to take the basic information of elementary and middle school science class and show your children how this information fits into everyday life.

Do your kids ever ask, "Why is this important? When will I ever need to know that again?" Well, chances are that it is important, but the beauty of the natural science gets hidden behind a lot of dry facts and figures. This book is designed to help you, as a parent, lead your child on a path of discovery. But, more importantly, it should help you both to appreciate and respect the natural world. Once that is in place, the desire to understand how things work will come on its own.

By sharing this knowledge with your children you will give them an invaluable gift of awareness and understanding of the world around them. Science isn't just for future doctors and engineers. Every citizen should have a basic understanding of how our world, and all our stuff, works. Try to make science a real part of your lives, because, well… it is.

This book is dedicated to my wonderful husband,

Dr. Robert Talanian.

Throughout my years of writing <u>Science for Parents</u>, he has been my constant advocate, a frequent mentor, an insightful editor, and, as always, my best friend.

Contents

The chapters in this book are grouped by subject area. It will be helpful to read the Physics chapter first, but feel free to skip around based on whatever you or your child has found an interest in. Some of the sections may be too full of unfamiliar information when you first read them, but keep circling back between chapters and sections as your kid's interests unfold. Many educators believe that the best way to learn scientific concepts is through "spiral learning". This means introducing the relatively easy-to-understand parts of a new concept first, then gradually introducing its more complex parts over time. By looping back to different chapters in this book, the idea that the basic laws of Nature hold true for all subsets of science will gradually unfold.

Physics – don't worry – it won't hurt! You probably already know more than you think you do. While physics isn't typically in elementary school syllabi, it really helps to understand some very basic principles before doing anything else.

- Everyday Example - Newton's First Law of Motion
- Everyday Knowledge - How To Win a Water Balloon Fight
- Everyday Activity - See in X-Ray Vision!
- Everyday Activity - Play With light
- Everyday Knowledge - Rainbows
- Everyday Knowledge - Fiber Optics
- Everyday Knowledge - The Sun
- Everyday Knowledge - Energy and the Human Body
- Everyday Knowledge - The B.T.U.
- Everyday Knowledge - Safer Roads

- Everyday Experiments - Temperature & Pressure 1, 2 and 3
- Everyday Knowledge - The Difference Between Soup & Stew
- Everyday Knowledge - Convection Ovens
- Everyday Experiment - Convection Can Be Pretty

Chemistry – Everything is made of chemicals. The basic components of absolutely everything, from cheese to chocolate, from skin cells to cell phones, from dust mites to the Dolomites, are atoms and molecules. This chapter provides a very brief introduction to seeing the world through the eyes of a chemist.

- Everyday Knowledge - Sugar
- Everyday Knowledge - Caveat Emptor
- Everyday Activity - Static Electricity
- Everyday Knowledge - Static Electricity
- Everyday Experiment - The Famous Kitchen Sink Volcano
- Everyday Knowledge - Food
- Everyday Experiment - Food
- Everyday Experiment - Clothing

Astronomy - puts our place in the Universe into context. Where did the Earth come from? How did it get to be the way it is? This chapter introduces the concept of the planet as a whole, and how Earth fits into the (really) big picture. You will learn about the solar system and the Milky Way Galaxy, and will be introduced to the universe in all its difficult to comprehend glory.

- Everyday Activity - View the Milky Way
- Everyday Knowledge - Solar Eclipse
- Everyday Activity - Moon Journal

Meteorology - brings together the studies of space, earth and water. How does the movement of the planet affect your weather? Why is it colder in the winter and warmer in the summer? Why is it hottest near the Equator?

- Everyday Experiment - A Mini Water Cycle in a Dish
- Everyday Knowledge - Clouds
- Everyday Activity - What Do Clouds Look Like?
- Everyday Example - Thunderstorms
- Everyday Knowledge - The Wind Tunnel Effect
- Everyday Knowledge - The Wind Chill Effect

Geology - lessons introduce the concept of the Earth as an ever-changing place. By studying rocks and minerals we can understand how different regions of our planet were formed and how they might change in the future.

- Everyday Activity - Sand Art
- Everyday Activity - Rocks Online
- Everyday Activity - Rocks in Real Life
- Everyday Activity - Play with Rocks
- Everyday Experiment - Mini-glaciers 1
- Everyday Experiment - Mini-glaciers 2
- Everyday Activity - Learn About Dirt

Life Science - Emphasis is on how Life got started, how form follows function, and how living things and non-living things come together to form an ecosystem. This teaches respect for the natural world and how everything works together, as well as an understanding of the inter-dependence of species. Also, this chapter provides an introduction to the study of organisms at their molecular level.

- Everyday Activity - Digital Archaeology
- Everyday Activity - Visualizing Mitosis & Meiosis
- Everyday Knowledge - Vaccines
- Everyday Knowledge - Antibiotics
- Everyday Knowledge - Bees
- Everyday Activity - See What You Can't See
- Everyday Knowledge - The Air We Breathe

Appendix of Metric System Units — A summary of some of the basic units of measurement used by scientists.

- Everyday Activity - Orders of Magnitude

PHYSICS

Many experts agree that kids should learn physics first, before any other scientific discipline. This "physics first" movement started in education decades ago, but, unfortunately, so many adults have scary or boring memories of their own physics classes that this idea rarely gets implemented in today's classrooms.

Most children understand physics at a holistic level. They understand intuitively that throwing a ball at an upward angle makes it go farther than throwing it straight. They expect heavier things to have more momentum than lighter things. At higher levels, physics is complicated, and requires knowledge of very advanced math to understand. But there are a few basic facts that everybody should be aware of, and these facts are simple and straightforward. What's more, once you know these facts, many other things become obvious. Once kids are comfortable with multiplication and division, the basic equations can be introduced. So let's get started!

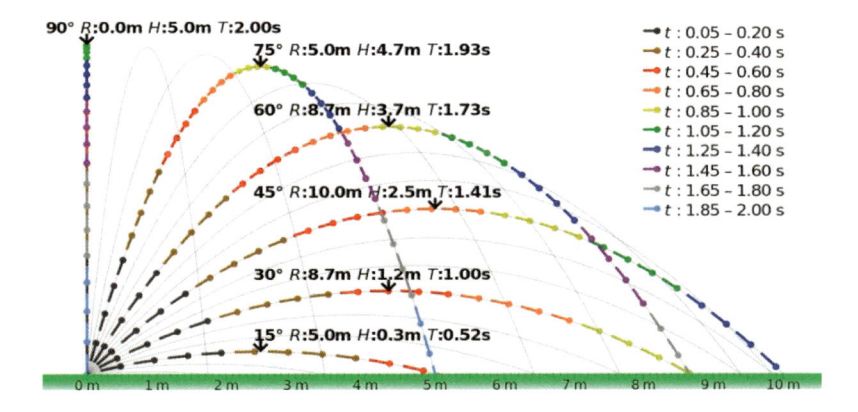

Graphic illustration of how an object thrown at a 45° angle from the ground will travel the farther than an object thrown at a lower or higher angle Image courtesy of CMGlee via www.commons.wikimedia.org/wiki/File:Ideal_projectile_motion_for_different_angles.svg

BASIC TERMS

There are some very basic words that need to be understood, and then everything else will go much more smoothly.

Matter   Anything that occupies space and has mass

Mass   The amount of matter in an object

Weight   An object's mass multiplied by the acceleration of gravity.

Since the acceleration of gravity on Earth is the same for all objects, we generally ignore this difference and use mass and weight interchangeably. But mass is a constant feature of an object, whereas weight can change in different environments. Your weight on the moon would be a lot less than your weight on Earth, because the moon has so much less gravity. But your mass would remain the same.

Volume   The amount of 3-dimensional space that an object occupies

Look at the fine print on a cereal box and find the words that say:

"This product is packaged by weight and not volume. Some settling of the contents may have occurred during shipment".

This simply means that the cereal company put a guaranteed amount (Mass) of product into the box, but, over time, the cereal settles down and it looks as if the box is only half full. This is a good way to show young kids the difference between these two scientific terms, and how the words are used in real life. It also provides a good lesson in being a savvy shopper — larger packages do not necessarily mean more stuff inside!

Density   The mass divided by the volume, d = m / V.

A golf ball is about the same size as a ping pong ball but much heavier. The golf ball has a higher density – it has much more mass taking up the same amount of space (volume).

Speed   The change in distance per unit of time. A car driving on a highway might have a speed of approximately 65 miles / 1 hour , or 65mph

Velocity   This is often used interchangeably with speed, but there is one very important difference: Velocity also indicates a direction. The car going 65 miles / hour has a speed. The same car driving **west** at 65 miles / hour has a velocity. To get really technical, a car driving due west at 65 miles/hour has an easterly velocity of -65 miles/hour. Its northerly and southerly velocities = 0. Think about it!

Acceleration   This is the change in speed or velocity divided by the change in time. In other words, acceleration is the *rate of change* of speed.

Consider a car starting up and accelerating from 0 miles/hour to 15 miles/hour in 3 seconds. Its speed increases during the course of those three seconds. The actual calculation requires math that kids won't learn until high school, but the concept of acceleration can be introduced much earlier. If a car is going 5 mph after the first second,

10 mph after the second second, and 15 mph after the third second, it is increasing its speed by 5 mph/second and this is its acceleration.

Acceleration can also be negative. When you apply the brakes in your car, its speed is decreasing, and so the rate of change of its speed is still its acceleration, only there would be a negative sign in front of that number.

Newton's Laws

Some Laws Cannot Be Broken!

Newton is often depicted in cartoons "discovering" gravity when an apple fell onto his head. As the legend goes, he sat up, rubbed his head, and said something like "Eureka! – everything seems to fall down toward the Earth, never up!" Actually, Newton was a lot more rigorous in his experiments, which culminated in his declaration of three basic laws of motion. In 1657 he published his findings in a book, *"Philosophiæ Naturalis Principia Mathematica"*. This work was extremely complex in the way he used math to prove his ideas; in fact, he invented Calculus to do so. But Newton worked hard so that we don't have to. All you need to know, and all your kids need to know at this point, is that these statements about force and motion are always true and these equations will work for any situation in everyday life. These truths are so basic that scientists simply refer to them as "Newton's Laws".

Newton's First Law - Law of Uniform Motion:

> An object in uniform motion will stay in that motion until some other force acts on it.

This was quite a radical idea in Newton's time. Because of gravity and friction, every object on Earth has invisible forces acting on it that effect its motion. If you slide a ball across a large, perfectly flat and smooth surface, the ball will eventually stop, apparently on its own. But there is an external force acting on it, and that force is friction. If you decrease the friction, maybe by lubricating the surface of the ball, it will take longer to stop. If you could somehow eliminate friction entirely, the ball would never stop. Newton proved mathematically that, in the absence of any external force, an object in uniform motion will maintain that uniform motion.

The Law of Inertia   A special case of the First Law

A body persists in its state of rest unless acted upon by an external force.   (Many parents of teenagers claim an especially keen understanding of this law.)

A book that is placed on a floor and never touched will never move on its own. While this seems so simple that it's not even worth stating, 300 years ago it needed to be proved. Newton's work mathematically proved that this would always be true.

Centrifugal Force   Another special case of Newton's First Law

As explained above, inertia is the tendency if an object in motion to stay in uniform motion. If you have a ball on a string and you spin it around in a circle, the moment you let go of the string the ball will shoot out in a straight line. It will not continue to spin in a circle. That's because at any given instant the ball is actually aiming in a straight line. Any point on its circular orbit can be considered as the starting point of a straight line leading away from the circle. Let go of the string, and the ball (the object in motion) continues on that uniform line of motion until some other force changes its course. This is often called centrifugal force, from the Latin words centrum (center) and fugere (to flee).

Centripetal Force

Again, imagine a ball on a string being spun in a circle. The ball's natural inclination would be to fly out in a straight line, as would happen if the person holding the string suddenly let it go. But, by holding onto the string, a centripetal force is applied, holding the ball in circular, rather than linear motion. This is from the Latin words centrum (center) and petere (to go towards). A good strategy for remembering this word is to think of a flower. The petals always attach at the center of the blossom.

Image courtesy of JJ Harrison via
www.commons.wikimedia.org/wiki/File:Erigeron_Glaucus.jpg

Everyday Example
Newton's First Law of Motion

Newton never rode in a car, but we do almost every day, and so we experience his first law every time the car moves out of a stopped position. When stopped at a traffic light, a car and the people inside it, are objects at rest. When the light turns green, the driver steps on the accelerator, and the car moves forward. The people in the car feel a backward push into their seat. There is, of course, nothing pushing the people backward, rather, it is the **inertia** of their bodies at rest. The car is moving forward because of its motor is accelerating, exerting a force on the road (through the tires) in the opposite direction. The people inside the car have no motor. It takes a little more time for them to catch up to the car.

Now imagine a car going forward at a constant speed. The driver suddenly steps on the brakes hard, forcing the car to an abrupt stop. The people in the car get pushed forward, yet there is no force pushing them forward. Their bodies are objects in motion that want to stay in that uniform motion. Hitting the brakes (or negative acceleration, in scientific terms) stops the car, but it takes a few seconds for the people to catch up.

When a car turns sharply to the left, the people in it feel as if they are getting shoved to the right. Next time this happens to you and your kids, try to shout above the cries of *"He/she is crushing me!!!!!"* and calmly explain the phenomenon of inertia. Just like the ball on a string experiences centrifugal force, their bodies are objects trying to stay in a uniform motion, which is a straight line.

Better yet - save the explanation for when you get home.

Newton's Second Law of Motion

Force = mass x acceleration   also written as   F = ma

This equation states that the force (F) of any object is equal to that object's mass (m) multiplied by the object's acceleration (a).

Imagine two balls of the same size – a kingpin bowling ball and a volleyball - rolling down a smooth hill. There is a small pile of stones at the bottom of this hill. Which ball will destroy the pile? The bowling ball has a mass of about 7 kilograms, or 7,000 grams. The volleyball has a mass of only about 230 grams. The balls are rolling down the same hill, and so have the same acceleration due to gravity. The mass of the bowling ball is about 30 times that of the volleyball, (7000 ÷ 230 = 30.4). Since their acceleration is the same, the **force** of the bowling ball is about 30 times greater.

Force of the bowling ball = 7.0 kg x 9.8 meters / sec^2 = 68.6 kg meters / sec^2.

Force of the volleyball = 0.23 kg x 9.8 meters / sec^2 = 2.25 kg meters / sec^2.

The idea of a heavier object having more force than a lighter object seems obvious. But Newton figured out why this is true mathematically, and eventually came up with this equation. This fact is so useful that scientists use the term "Newton" as the unit of force, the way we use the word "minute" to describe a unit of time.

A Newton is defined as = 1 kilogram X 1 meter / sec^2

Newton also identified the numerical value for the Earth's gravity to be:

9.8 meters / sec^2 or   32 feet / sec^2.

Note the units, which show that this number is actually the ***acceleration*** due to the force of gravity, not the force of gravity. We generally abbreviate this to the "force" of gravity, but that is technically incorrect. Read on to learn why.

Anything that is dropped will fall to the ground at the same acceleration. It's counter-intuitive, but true. In the above example, the bowling ball and the volleyball will reach the bottom of the hill at the same moment, but if they hit another object (a wall, or someone's foot) the bowling ball will hit with a lot more force. If you stand on bridge and drop a spoon and a chair, common sense tells us that the chair will reach the ground first. But it won't. The math to

A word of caution here:
As is often the case when explaining scientific phenomena, there are other, complicating factors involved. Nice, neat mathematical explanations might not appear correct in the real world. If one were to drop a hammer and a feather from a bridge, chances are very good that the hammer would reach the ground long before the feather. Does that contradict everything written above? No. It's just that other factors, like wind or air resistance or friction, can have very noticeable effects on these kinds of experiments. In 1971 the astronaut David Scott tried this experiment by dropping a hammer and a feather from his hands onto the surface of the moon and achieved the mathematically predicted results. Since there is no air or wind on the moon, his experiment was free from many of the Earth's complicating factors. www.youtube.com/watch?v=4mTsrRZEMwA

explain this is complicated. Basically it involves pitting the mass of the planet Earth itself against the mass of whatever objects you choose to drop off the bridge. In other words, you would have to drop something close to the mass of the Earth itself to see a difference in the rate of falling! While this won't happen in everyday life, you can imagine how equations about gravity would come in handy for astronomers who study the interactions between stars.

Momentum is often used interchangeably with force in everyday language, but there is a mathematical distinction. Momentum is defined as the mass of an object, m, multiplied by its velocity, v.

$$M = mv$$

(Note a lower case m always implies mass; the upper case M implies momentum.)

Since F = ma and a = v/t then F = mv/t and Ft = mv = M, and **Ft = M.**

In plain English, this means that the force of an object (F) multiplied by the time the force is applied (t) is equal to its momentum (M).

The mass is constant, and an object thrown with a given velocity has that velocity. So momentum (mass x velocity) must be the same, regardless of time. However, if the time of contact is shorter, then the force must be greater. If the time of contact is longer, then the force will decrease. See below for a real world example.

> ## *Everyday Knowledge –*
> ## *How to Win a Water Balloon Fight*
>
> If someone throws a water balloon to you, and you hold out your hand to stop it, the water balloon will crash and burst onto your rigid hand. It is in contact with your hand for a very short time, t and so the force, F, is greater. If, instead, you try to gently catch the balloon and swing your hand to continue the trajectory of the balloon, you will be able to hold it intact, and, of course, be able to lob it back at your opponent!
>
> In this case, the *time* of contact is longer, and so, proportionally, the force is less. Think about it!

NEWTON'S THIRD LAW OF MOTION

For every action there is an equal and opposite reaction.

This is even truer in physics than in human relations. Whenever an object exerts a force on another object, the second object simultaneously exerts a force back onto the first in the opposite direction. The easiest way to experience this law is while treading water in a pool or pond. If two people put their palms together and push with an equal force, both people will get pushed away from each other. What will not happen is one person staying still and the other moving away.

Of course the same phenomenon happens when a single swimmer pushes off the side of a pool. The swimmer accelerates forward. The pool doesn't move, but that is because the pool's mass is many orders of magnitude greater than the mass of the swimmer.

There they are – the three most basic laws of Newtonian physics.
Not really all that scary when you think about it, right?

If you teach your kids these basic rules, they will have a much easier time approaching many other scientific ideas that they will face down the road, and be more successful at water balloon fights!

> *Newton earned his fame because he proved, through a lot of hard work, some of the most fundamental truths about the way things work. Some things make sense, like the fact that a truck crashing into a wall will do more damage than a bicycle crashing into the same wall. Other things don't necessarily make sense at first glance, like the fact that heavy things fall at the same speed as lighter things. Newton discovered some very complicated mathematical proofs that showed how all objects would obey these basic rules and now these mathematical tools can be used to accurately predict force and motion over a variety of conditions. These equations form the basics of all science.*

Electromagnetism

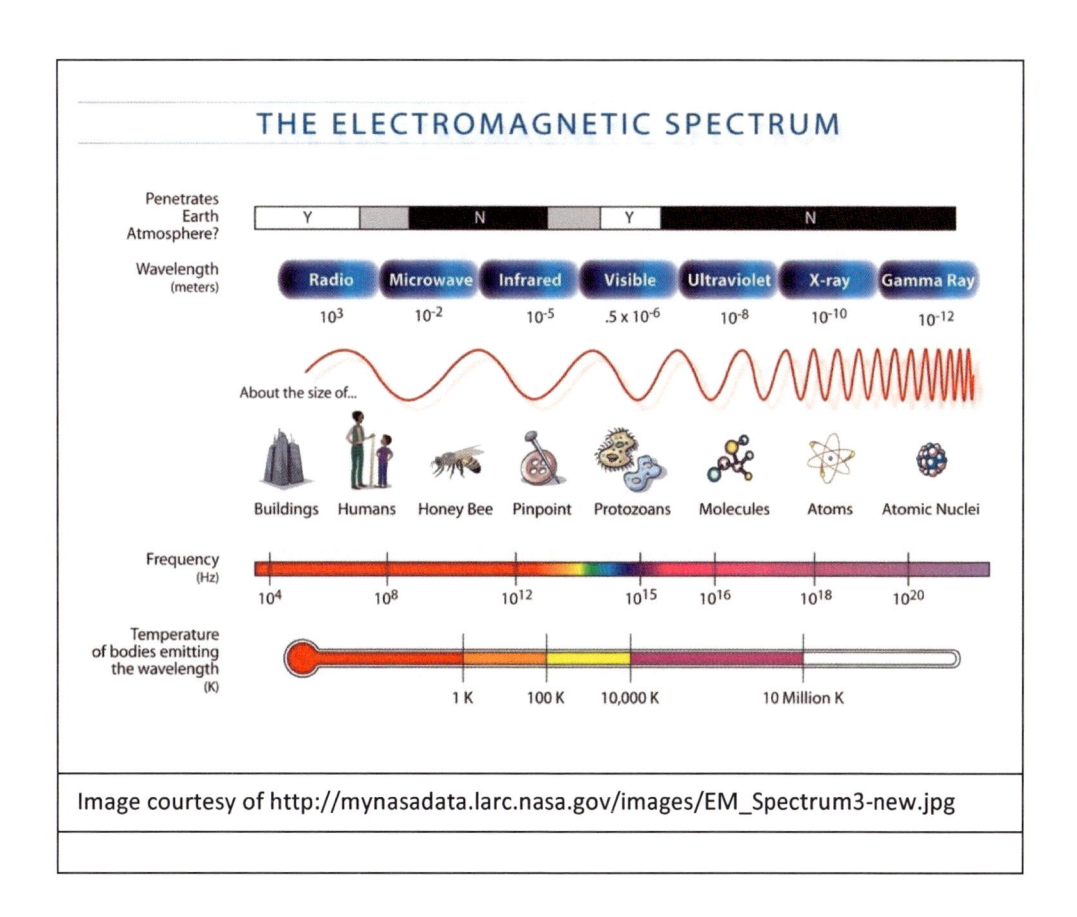

THE ELECTROMAGNETIC SPECTRUM

Penetrates Earth Atmosphere? Y / N / Y / N

Wavelength (meters):
- Radio: 10^3
- Microwave: 10^{-2}
- Infrared: 10^{-5}
- Visible: $.5 \times 10^{-6}$
- Ultraviolet: 10^{-8}
- X-ray: 10^{-10}
- Gamma Ray: 10^{-12}

About the size of…
Buildings, Humans, Honey Bee, Pinpoint, Protozoans, Molecules, Atoms, Atomic Nuclei

Frequency (Hz): 10^4, 10^8, 10^{12}, 10^{15}, 10^{16}, 10^{18}, 10^{20}

Temperature of bodies emitting the wavelength (K): 1 K, 100 K, 10,000 K, 10 Million K

Image courtesy of http://mynasadata.larc.nasa.gov/images/EM_Spectrum3-new.jpg

The electromagnetic spectrum includes all types of radiation, including visible light, microwaves, radio waves, and X-rays. It exists everywhere, on Earth and in outer space. Every time you cook food in a microwave, listen to the radio, get an X-ray of a broken bone, warm yourself in the Sun, or just look at something, you are using the electromagnetic spectrum.

It's easy to understand the terms "wavelength" and "frequency" by imagining waves at a beach, on a day when waves are breaking on the shore at a fairly regular rate.

The wavelength is simply the length, or distance, between the very top of one wave to the very top of the next wave. When dealing with ocean waves, the wavelength would be measured in feet, or meters. When dealing with things like X-rays, the distance between each wave is much, much smaller, on the order of 0.1 nanometers. That's 10^{-10} meters, or about 0.0000000004 inches!

The frequency is the speed at which the waves follow each other. Wavelength and frequency have an inverse relationship. This means that longer wavelengths have slower frequencies, and shorter wavelengths have faster (higher) frequencies. It takes longer for large waves to complete a cycle, while tiny waves can move extremely fast.

> The unit of frequency is the **Hertz (Hz)** which is defined as the number of wave cycles per second. This was named in honor of a German physicist, Heinrich Hertz, who made many important discoveries about radiation and electromagnetism during the latter half of the 19th century.

Going back to the example of waves on a beach, imagine the waves coming at intervals of about 10 seconds. In other words, every 10 seconds another wave would crash on the sand. In scientific terms the frequency would be written as 1 cycle / 10 seconds, or 1 ÷ 10 which is 0.10 Hertz.

Higher frequency (shorter wavelength) radiation has more energy than lower frequency (longer wavelength) radiation. The wavelengths between the radio waves that transmit sound from a radio or television station to your home are on the order of about 1,000 meters. Their frequency is about 10^4 or 10,000 Hz. You can listen to the radio all day, every day, without any physical effects on your body. Compare that with being exposed for just a couple of hours to ultraviolet rays from the sun, which have a frequency of about 10^{16} Hz, or 10,000,000,000,000,000 cycles per second! Most humans will be physically burned by the energy that these rays contain. Even so, ultraviolet rays are much lower in energy when compared to X-rays, which cycle at about 10^{18} Hz, or 1,000,000,000,000,000,000 cycles per second!

Everyday Activity - See in X-Ray Vision!

NASA currently uses different telescopes to "see" what is out there in the cosmos. The Hubble Telescope took many iconic pictures of things in several spectral ranges, including the visible range. The Spitzer Telescope records things that display in the infrared range and the Chandra Telescope "sees" X-rays. The Webb Telescope, which will be in geostationary orbit 1.5 million kilometers (about 930,060 miles) from Earth, will look in the infrared range. For more information, and to see some incredibly beautiful images, go to the websites for each project.

www.hubblesite.org/

www.jwst.nasa.gov/

www.spitzer.caltech.edu/

www.chandra.harvard.edu/

http://coolcosmos.ipac.caltech.edu/

By getting data from different wavelengths, scientists get more puzzle pieces to work with. The more data that they get, the more accurate their knowledge about different stars and planets and galaxies will be.

LIGHT

What we refer to as "light" is a specific range of electromagnetic wavelengths that human eyes are able to detect. Electromagnetic radiation with wavelengths between 400 and 700 nanometers can be seen with human eyes. As discussed in the previous section, the entire electromagnetic spectrum includes radiation with wavelengths from 6000 kilometers (radio waves) down to 0.03 nanometers (gamma-rays), so what we can see with our eyes is a very tiny fraction of what's really out there. That's why astronomers use telescopes that can "see" microwaves and radio waves and X-rays in addition to regular light telescopes. Doctors use X-rays to "see" what is inside our bodies.

Visible light includes all the colors we can see. We can see separate colors because our eyes have evolved to be able to receive and distinguish between light of particular wavelengths. White light is actually a mixture of different colors of light.

Each color has its own particular wavelength in the Electromagnetic Spectrum.

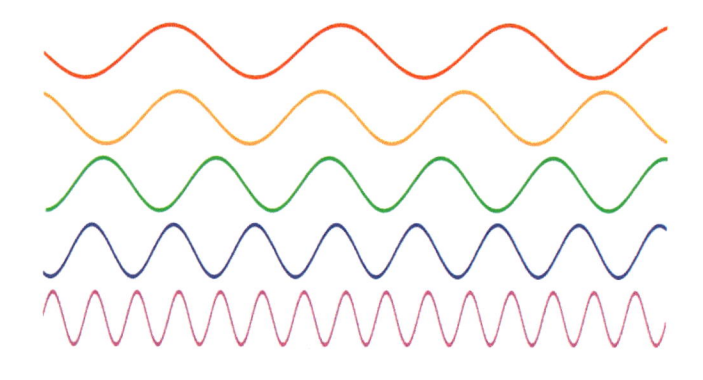

Image courtesy of Wikipedia commons:
www.commons.wikimedia.org/wiki/File:Sine_waves_different_frequencies.svg

Red	700 nanometers
Orange	620 nanometers
Yellow	580 nanometers
Green	530 nanometers
Blue	475 nanometers
Indigo	450 nanometers
Violet	400 nanometers

We see **colors** because different materials absorb and reflect different wavelengths of light. A green leaf contains chemicals that **absorb** light in the blue-ish and red-ish ends of the spectrum, and **reflect** wavelengths around 530 nanometers. These wavelengths are then received by our eyes and so our brains register the leaf as being green. *When the color of a material is changed, whether by a crayon on a piece of paper, paint on a house or dye on your hair, the chemical structure of the outermost layers is actually changed. The new chemical structure absorbs and reflects different wavelengths of light than the old chemical structure did, and so our eyes "see" that as a change in the material's color.*

Light can be reflected or refracted.

Reflection is the phenomenon of light bouncing off a reflective surface, such as a mirror or the surface of water. Light will always reflect at an angle equal to the angle of incidence, which is the angle at which it hit the surface. It's the same principle used in playing pool. When a ball bounces off the side of a pool table, it always bounces off at an angle equal to the angle that it hit the wall at. *Always.* Light reflection works the same way.

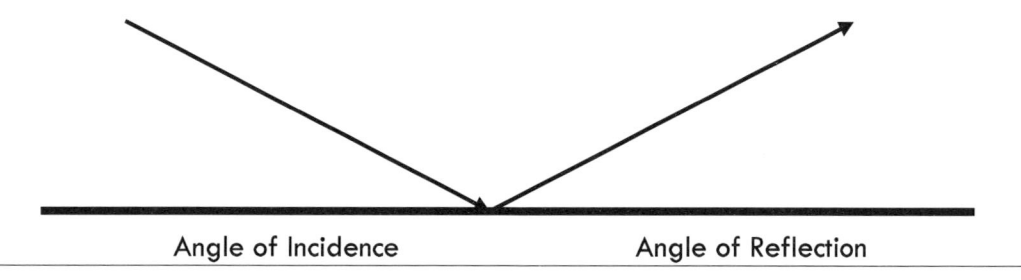

| Angle of Incidence | Angle of Reflection |

> ## *Everyday Knowledge - Fiber Optics*
>
> Chances are that the images you watch on TV and the pages you view on the web are brought to you by the transmission of light through fiber optic cables. These are extremely thin tubes of glass that "carry" light over miles and miles, and are able to retain an accurate representation of those images, bringing them right into your home. Fiber optic cables work because light signals bounce off the insides of the fibers at low incident angles very efficiently, and very, very quickly.

Refraction is the apparent bending of light. This is easy to illustrate with a drinking straw or a pencil in a clear glass of water. When you look through the glass at the straw, the straw appears to be bent. That's because light travels through the water more slowly than it travels through air, and so the image your eyes perceive is distorted.

The **"Refractive Index"** of any substance is the ratio of the speed of light travelling through a perfect vacuum divided by the speed of light travelling through that substance. Every substance has its own Refractive Index (RI), and this is a defining characteristic of that substance. Under the same conditions this number will always be the same. The RI of light through air is very close to 1, meaning that it is very close to the speed of light through a vacuum. The refractive index of water is 1.33. The RI of glass ranges around 1.5, depending on the particular type of glass. Diamonds have a very high refractive index of 2.4, which explains their beauty. Diamond itself will bend (refract) light a great deal, and an expertly cut diamond will receive and refract light at many different angles, resulting is that much sought after sparkle.

A regular diagonal stripe pattern is refracted by a curved glass of water in this very impressive depiction of refraction

Photo courtesy of Mark Oakley **via** www.flickr.com/photos/mrmoaks/7788291338/

Creative commons usage

The angle at which light is refracted is dependent upon its wavelength, and so the component colors of light each refract at slightly different angles. Thus the colors become separated (dispersed) and this phenomenon is called **dispersion**. Rainbows occur when water droplets in the sky split the electromagnetic radiation of sunlight into its component wavelengths. As sunlight shines into a cloud of mist, the sun's rays are refracted (bent), then reflected back, but cannot leave the water droplet without being refracted again.

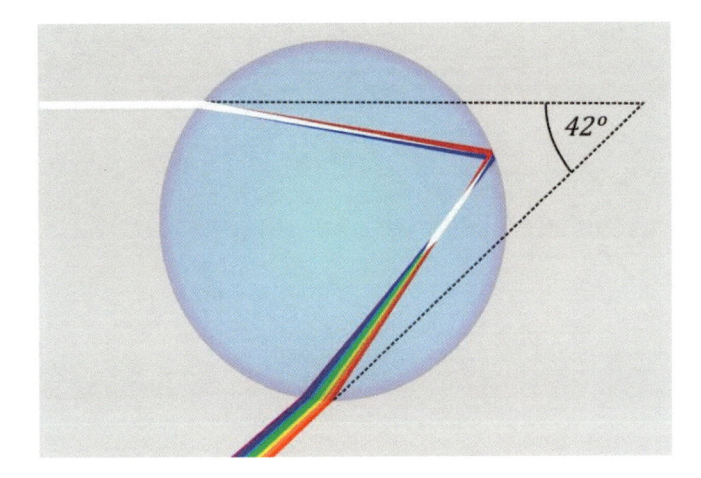

Refraction and reflection in a raindrop, producing a rainbow. White light separates into different colors (wavelengths) on entering the raindrop, as red light is refracted by a lesser angle than blue light. On leaving the raindrop, the red rays have turned through a smaller angle than the blue rays, producing a rainbow.

Image courtesy of KES47 via http://commons.wikimedia.org/wiki/File:Rainbow1.svg

As white light enters each individual raindrop, it gets reflected back out of the raindrop, at a specific angle, 40° at the violet end of the spectrum, through 42° at the red end. After reflection the light must pass back out through the water droplet, but in doing so the water refracts the white light, splitting the colors by their own wavelengths. It exits the droplet at a 138° angle. The colors will always appear in the same order by their wavelengths, and the order can be remembered using the mnemonic device "Roy G Biv", which stands for Red-Orange-Yellow-Green-Blue-Indigo-Violet.

Image courtesy of Eric Rolph via www.commons.wikimedia.org/wiki/File:Double-alaskan-rainbow-airbrushed.jpg

> ## Everyday Knowledge – Rainbows
>
> You can only view a rainbow if the sun is behind you, because you are witnessing the sun's light shining into individual water droplets and being reflected back towards the sun. Therefore you cannot see a rainbow if the sun is in front of you. Red is always the color on the outside of the arc, and violet is always the color on the inside of the arc.
>
> We see rainbows as arches, but they are actually circular. It's just that the bottom half of the circle is below the horizon.

More handy definitions in optics are:

Transparent – a substance that light can pass through

Opaque – a substance that light cannot pass through

Photon – A discreet packet of electromagnetic energy in the visible part of the spectrum. For centuries philosophers and scientists debated whether light was a particle or a wave. In the early 20th century, scientists decided that it is both. Light actually displays characteristics of both particulate matter and wave energy.

Speed of Light – Light travels at 186,000 miles / second, or in metric terms, 300,000 kilometers / second. This is the value for travel through a vacuum, and through outer space, where there is no air. Its speed is slower through air and even slower through water, which accounts for the phenomenon of refraction, described above.

Light Year – The distance that light will travel in 365 days at 186,000 miles per second.   One light year = 5.88×10^{12} miles or 9.46×10^{15} meters.

Everyday Activity – Play With light

A **prism** is a piece of glass that can split white light into its component colored lights. This process of splitting light into colors is called **dispersion**. Prisms are fun to play with and can be purchased in any number of places, in hobby stores on through online scientific suppliers or educational toy retailers.

Everyday Knowledge – the Sun

The sun's radiation is composed of:

40% at wavelengths of infrared (IR) or longer
50% at wavelengths in the visible range
10% at wavelengths in the ultraviolet (UV)

It's the UV rays that cause sunburn - remember these have a much higher energy and therefore can penetrate skin while the others do not have enough energy to do so. Both UVA and UVB rays are dangerous. UVB energy causes the familiar redness of sunburn, because they affect the epidermis (skin's outer layer).

The UVA rays actually do their damage at a deeper skin level called the dermis, and can cause invisible, but very real, damage to dermal cells. This damage can include initial redness and swelling due to inflammation, but also can cause long-term damage to the DNA in these cells, eventually leading to cancer.

Energy

The term "energy" is defined as the capacity to do work. "Work" doesn't have to be useful by this definition; it is just the transfer of energy. Energy can be stored and used in many forms. There are several types of energy with examples that everyone can relate to:

Potential – it's there but not being used at the moment, e.g., a ball balanced on top of a hill, or a teenager lying on the couch;

Kinetic – in motion, e.g. a ball rolling across a floor, water flowing through a dam, or a person dancing;

Chemical – potential energy is stored within the bonds between different atoms in a molecule. When these atoms and molecules break apart or combine with other molecules chemical energy will be consumed or generated;

Thermal – a hot mug of tea has more thermal energy than does a cold glass of water (and a large mug of hot tea has more thermal energy than a tiny tea cup of hot tea);

Electrical – a battery in a flashlight has potential electrical energy, but when the flashlight is turned on, the flow of electrons from the battery towards the light bulb is electrical energy;

Light – when those electrons reach a light bulb, their energy is given off as light

Forms of energy are often linked. For example, as wood burns it gives off both heat and light energy. Modern, "energy efficient" light bulbs are designed to emit more light energy and less heat energy with the same, or less, input of electrical energy.

From a personal standpoint, when sitting down, your body has the potential to do work. Playing soccer, your body is using chemical energy obtained from the breakdown of the food you've eaten to create kinetic energy.

Thermal Energy, a.k.a. Heat

Heat is something that every human thinks they instinctively understand. But when heat is studied scientifically, a redefining of some basic principles is in order. First of all, cold is just the relative lack of heat. "Cold" doesn't exist; it is only less heat. Since cold doesn't have any properties of its own, it can't travel. When you put ice cubes in a glass of warm water, the water molecules close to the ice cubes are cooled down (their kinetic energy is reduced) by the ice absorbing the heat from the water, not because of the water absorbing cold from the ice. The end result is essentially the same — the contents of the glass are achieving **thermal equilibrium**, meaning everything in the glass is getting to the same temperature. But, thinking like a scientist, it is the water's heat melting the ice, and not the ice's cold cooling the water. Likewise, on a very hot day, sitting with your back against a stone wall feels good because some of the heat from your body is being transferred to the wall; the wall is not bestowing a gift of coldness to your body.

What is Heat, anyway?

Heat is a form of energy. It can be expressed as a quantity, and so is measureable. Heat can be transferred from one body to another.

Why do some things heat up more than others?

Every substance has its own **Specific Heat Capacity**, which is as much a defining part of that substance as its color, hardness, boiling point, or other physical descriptor. It is the energy required to raise the temperature of a defined unit of a substance by 1 degree. The amount of heat an object has is therefore a function of its own specific heat capacity (its capacity to get and retain heat) and the source of that heat, which could be anything from sunlight, to a flame on the stove, to the generation of heat by a motor or other device attached to it.

Who cares?

One example of how knowledge of a material's specific heat capacity is useful would be the construction of pots & pans. High quality cooking pans are made using different metals for the bottom, which comes into direct contact with the source of heat, and the handle, which comes into contact with the cook's hands. The bottom should be made of a metal with a high heat capacity, to hold as much heat as possible next to the food. Handles should always be made of a material with a very low heat capacity, as these would stay relatively cool to the touch even when the pot itself gets very hot.

Who Else Cares?

Housing construction also makes use of this sort of knowledge. Some building materials retain heat better than others. If you live in an area with wide fluctuations in the daily temperature range, like the desert southwest of the United States, then you want your home to be built out of a material with a high specific heat capacity. Materials like adobe hold onto the sun's heat during the day, keeping the interior of the house cool, but gradually release this stored heat as outside temperatures drop overnight, thus keeping the inhabitants warm.

Everyday Knowledge

Energy & the Human Body

Here's a little information to make this whole concept a bit more up close and personal:

A calorie is the amount of energy it takes to heat 1 gram of water by 1° Celsius.

This is the Specific Heat Capacity of water. There are about 5 grams of water in a teaspoon, so you are dealing here with about 1/5 of a teaspoon of water. It takes 1 calorie to raise that water's temperature exactly 1 degree Celsius.

This term useful for scientific experiments, but in everyday language the **Calorie** (with a capital C) as used for food and diets, is actually a **kilocalorie**, that is 1,000 calories.

You consume Calories by eating food. The food has potential energy, which is stored in the chemical bonds of the molecules that make up the food, and these Calories provide your body with the energy to live. When you consume more Calories than you use, the extra – *potential* –energy is stored in your body in the chemical bonds of particular hydrocarbon molecules known as fat.

Note that it is the chemical energy of the bonds in the food's molecules that supplies you with energy to live, not the actual atoms of carbon, oxygen, etc. Those atoms are used to make more you, or to replace and renew the building blocks of your skin, organs, etc. The energy required to breathe, pump blood, and ride a bike comes from the bonds that hold the food's molecules together.

Why is fat so fattening? A gram of carbohydrate (like sugar or starch) provides 4 Calories and a gram of protein (like lean meat or fish) also supplies 4 Calories. But a gram of fat (like butter or oil or animal fat) supplies 9 Calories. Why? Because the bonds between carbon (and other) atoms in fat molecules are slightly different from those in carbs and protein, and they hold more energy. When your body breaks down these fat molecules, there is a net gain of energy and this energy is either used to do work (i.e. exercise) or is stored (as other fat molecules) in your body.

Heat energy is a subset of kinetic energy – the energy of motion. So how does a pot of hot water have more "motion" than a pot of cold water?

The answer is molecular motion. Another term for molecular motion is Brownian Motion. **This is the basis of all heat.**

For example, think about heating a pot of water on the stove. The chemical formula for water is H_2O. This molecule consists of one atom of oxygen that is connected to two atoms of hydrogen. The molecule forms a wide V shape, with the oxygen in the center, and the hydrogen atoms attached on either side of the oxygen. While easy to imagine this triangular shape, in reality this molecule is not a rigid triangle. Rather, the atoms in each individual molecule are in constant motion, vibrating with respect to each other. In a liquid state, these molecules are constantly moving closer or farther from each other. **Don't think of these molecules as being *in* a liquid. The molecules *are* the liquid.** When energy is added to water, for example, by turning the stove on, these

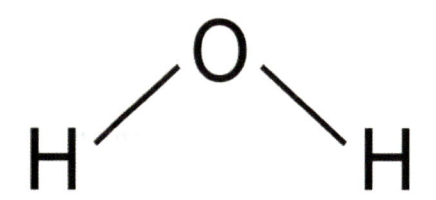

Everyday Knowledge – the B·T·U·

A common term used to describe heat is the British Thermal Unit, or **BTU**. If you have purchased a furnace or other heating appliance, it probably was advertised as being capable of putting out some number of BTU's. 1 BTU = the amount of energy it takes to raise the temperature of 1 pound of water by 1° Fahrenheit.

molecules move faster. More heat equals faster motion. The longer the pot is on the stove, the more heat is transferred from the stove to the water, and the faster those molecules will move. They quiver and shake faster and faster until they are moving so fast that the entire mass of water seems to move. The water is now "boiling" and large bubbles start to form. At this point – "the boiling point" – some of the molecules are moving so fast that they actually change from liquid to gas and escape from the pot as steam. This is called a **phase change** – the changing of matter (in this case, water) from one phase (liquid) into another (gas). The temperature at which this will happen is 212° Fahrenheit (100° Celsius). The boiling point of water will always be this temperature. In fact, all liquids have a specific boiling point and this is considered to be a defining property of each substance. No matter how long you boil water, or how rapidly the bubbles are forming, the temperature of the water will not get higher than its boiling point.

The opposite happens when water is poured into an ice cube tray and put in a freezer. The heat in the water gets transferred to the surrounding air in the freezer. That's why the back of a refrigerator is always warm: the refrigerator is removing heat from the food inside. As this heat is transferred out of the water, the water molecules move more and more slowly. When the temperature of the water in the tray gets to 32° F (0°C), those V-shaped water molecules are moving so slowly that they freeze. This means that they line up in such a pattern that the molecules hold onto each other and form a solid piece of water, otherwise known as ice. This is another example of a phase change; in this case matter is changed from its liquid phase to its solid phase.

> **Absolute Zero** is a super-cold state in which no molecules are moving at all. This temperature has been approached only under very sophisticated laboratory conditions. This state is defined as 0° Kelvin, which is equal to -273.15° Celsius or -458° Fahrenheit.

> *Everyday Knowledge - Safer Roads*
>
> When other chemicals are added to pure water, the water's freezing point and melting point are lowered. Even shallow salt water bays will stay liquid under colder temperatures while nearby fresh water ponds are frozen. This is because the presence of the NaCl ions disrupts the cozy lattice that the H_2O molecules are trying to freeze into. That's also why we use salt crystals to melt ice on roads and sidewalks in the winter. It must be colder for salted ice to stay frozen. Under most winter conditions, this change is enough to melt ice and make these surfaces safer.

Temperature, Volume & Pressure

This may sound intimidating, but hang on. The relationship between these three factors will be mentioned again and again in this book, in almost every chapter. It's that good.

Basically, temperature is a numerical measure of the amount of heat something has.

Volume is the amount of space something takes up.

Mathematically, the volume of a non-curved shape is: its length x its width x its depth.

$$V = L \times W \times D$$

Formulae that describe the volume of curved spaces can easily be looked up. For a sphere, $V = (4/3) \pi r^3$. Each unique shape has its own formula.

Pressure is harder to imagine, but just think of high pressure in an inflated balloon or tire.

Pressure is the force applied by a substance across the surface area it is bound by, Mathematically, $P = F \div A$

Since weight is a force, and $F = ma$ (Force = the mass of an object x its acceleration) we can usually simplify this equation to use an object's weight instead of its mass, as an object's weight here on Earth is its mass multiplied by the acceleration due to gravity.

There is a very important relationship between Temperature, Volume and Pressure: Pressure multiplied by Volume is always proportional to Temperature.

$$PV = nRT$$

The n and R refer to mathematic constants. When scientists measure these quantities to get accurate numerical answers, they have to be very careful in choosing units of measurement and doing the measuring. But, for everyday purposes, the concept of proportion is key.   Pressure x Volume will always *be proportional to* Volume:

$$PV \propto T.$$

- If temperature increases, pressure will also increase, as long as the volume stays the same.

Think of a fully inflated balloon. What happens when it gets too close to a lamp? It pops, because the heat from the light bulb causes an increase in temperature, which causes an increase in the pressure of the gas inside the balloon. Since it's already fully inflated, its volume can't increase, therefore the gas forces itself out (to increase the available volume) and, in doing so, makes a child cry.

- If temperature decreases, pressure will also decrease, as long as the volume stays the same.

Think of a cheap plastic water bottle. If you fill it with hot tap water and screw the cap on tightly, then place the bottle in the freezer. After a while, (about 30 minutes should do) the decrease in temperature causes a decrease in pressure and so it actually pulls a vacuum. You will see the sides of the bottle actually sucked inside, reducing the volume of the bottle a bit

Courtesy of Kristopha Hohn via Flickr and creative commons license
https://www.flickr.com/photos/seishin17/9696688130/

in response to these conditions.

- If temperature stays the same and the volume increases, the pressure will decrease.

- If temperature stays the same and the volume decreases, the pressure will increase.

This relationship will be revisited in every chapter from meteorology to geology.

Everyday Experiment

Temperature & Pressure 1

Take a clean, empty water or soda bottle. Either plastic or glass will do, but find a bottle with an opening that is the same size as a nickel or a quarter. Rinse the bottle opening, the coin, and your hands under cold running water (to cool them) and then place the coin over the bottle so that it covers the bottle opening with no air space visible. Hold the bottle and coin in a large pot in the kitchen sink. Run the hot water until it gets warm. Once warm water is running out, direct this stream into the pot. Remember to hold the bottle steady! Watch the coin closely. The warm water in the pot will raise the temperature of the air inside the bottle. This increase in temperature causes an increase in pressure inside the bottle, which causes the coin to pop up, thereby releasing this increased pressure.

Everyday Experiment
Temperature & Pressure 2

If you have two *identical* sauce pots, fill each with the exact same amount of water. To make sure the water is the same temperature, put the total amount needed in the refrigerator overnight. Put these pots on the stove and turn the heat on them to the same level. Cover one pot tightly and leave the other pot open. Which pot's water comes to a boil first? If you only have one pot, do the experiment twice and record how long it takes water to boil with and without a lid. Make sure the water comes directly from the fridge into the pot to insure that the temperature is the same to start. In both cases the pot itself should be room temperature at the beginning.

When the lid is off you increase the volume, thereby decreasing the pressure. Lower pressure corresponds to lower temperature, thus increasing the time it takes for the temperature to reach the boiling point. This could be the origin of the saying "A watched pot never boils". Watching the *pot* makes no difference, but watching the *water* does.

For most of the populated regions of the world, atmospheric pressure is the same, and referred to as "standard atmospheric pressure". In higher elevations the atmospheric pressure is reduced. The boiling point of pure water in Denver, Colorado is actually 95° C, instead of 100° C, and so recipes and cooking times often need to be adjusted for higher elevations. To ensure that food is cooked thoroughly.

Everyday Experiment
Temperature & Pressure 3

OK, this is not so much an experiment as an explanation. Every kid loves to shake a can of soda and then let an unsuspecting friend (or parent!) open it, right? We all know what happens, but why does it happen? The answer lies again in **PV ∝ T**.

When the can is shaken, kinetic energy is transferred from the shaker's hand to the molecules of soda in the can; because energy is always conserved (it never just goes away). Since these molecules are now moving faster the temperature of the soda as a whole increases. As long as the can is unopened, there is no increase in volume, and so the pressure also increases. When the can is popped open this high pressure situation causes an explosion into the face on an unsuspecting person.

If the soda is allowed to settle back down, the temperature will eventually decrease, thereby lowering the pressure. The can will be safe to open in a while. Exactly how long depends on the environment. It will take a long time if it's sitting in the sun, and a shorter time if left in the fridge.

There are three ways that heat can travel:

- Conduction - This is the transfer of heat energy from an area of faster molecular motion to an area of lesser molecular motion. Going back to the ice cubes in water model, molecules in the liquid water are moving much faster than the molecules of frozen water (ice). When the ice is put in the water, the faster-moving liquid molecules bump into the colder, slower, crystallized molecules at the edges of the ice cube. This gets the molecules at the edges of the ice cube moving faster (joining into the dance party, so to speak) and so they melt away and become liquid themselves. The process continues until all the molecules are at an equal temperature. (Eventually the temperature of the water will reach the temperature of the room. In a comfortably warm room, say $75°$ F, the water will eventually reach $75°$ too. Outside on a cold day the water will eventually reach the outdoor temperature. If that is about freezing, or $32°$ F, the water will become a slurry of ice particles in liquid water.) In scientific terms, this is called reaching thermal equilibrium.

- Radiation – This transfer of heat does not involve contact between two objects of higher and lower heat. A camp fire or a space heater warms the people sitting around it by radiative heat. Molecules in the hot object are moving so rapidly that charged atomic particles are created. These charged particles are converted to electromagnetic radiation. Unlike light waves and X-rays (described in the next section), heat waves exist at many different frequencies, and so occupy a relatively broad range of the electromagnetic spectrum illustration, although this is centered in the infrared.

- Convection – This is the upward movement of warmer matter into the space occupied by colder matter. Everyone knows the saying "heat rises", right? Why does heat rise? Let's use the example of water in a pot again. Take a pot full of cold water and place it on a stove. Turn the heat on and the water near the bottom of the pot gets warmed faster than the water near the top. Eventually all the water will be at the same temperature, but this is because of the process of convection. When the heat is turned on, the water molecules near the bottom of the pot start to move faster. As they move faster, there is no increase in the number of water molecules, but because of their fast movement, the same number of molecules takes up more volume. Remember, density = mass / volume, so, by definition, the warmer water becomes slightly less dense than the colder water, where the molecules are moving at a relatively slower pace.

> To illustrate this concept of molecular density, imagine a roomful of toddlers. Each child represents one molecule. During snack time, they all sit at a table in a relatively small space. Here there is a higher density of children. At recess, the same number of children run around frantically and takes up the entire room. The number of children hasn't increased, but they now occupy a much larger volume of space. Their density has decreased.

Same # of molecules in a smaller space = Higher density

Same # of molecules in a larger space = Lower density

Since the less dense, faster moving water is lighter then the denser, slower moving water, it rises to the top of the pot. As the warmer molecules rise to the top, they displace the colder molecules, which then are forced to sink to the bottom. As these colder molecules get close to the source of the heat, they start to move faster, become less dense, and rise to the top. The process continues.

Everyday Knowledge –

The Difference Between Soup & Stew

This is also why it is more important to frequently stir a pot of stew cooking on the stove, than it is to stir a pot of soup. Soup, being relatively thin and liquidy, can rely on the natural convection to move the various molecules around. Stew, being thicker, cannot move as easily. The molecules at the bottom of the pot cannot easily rise, and so those on the top cannot sink. The results can be a burnt bottom layer, and a cold top layer of stew.

Everyday Knowledge –

Convection ovens

In a convection oven, a fan circulates air, keeping the temperature inside the oven more even.

Let's say you put a casserole from the refrigerator into a regular oven. The cold casserole will maintain a thin layer of cold (or cooler) air around itself for a long time, even though the rest of the oven is relatively much warmer. If the same casserole is placed into a convection oven, the oven's fan constantly blows the air around, disrupting that layer of cooler air around the casserole, and allowing hot air to come in contact with the food.

This is why convection ovens typically cook food faster or at a lower temperature than do regular ovens.

Everyday Experiment –
Convection can be pretty

Convection is an easy phenomenon to illustrate using stuff you've probably already got in your kitchen.

> Clear Pyrex® pan – loaf size or 9" circular types are good
> Vegetable Oil
> Spices – e.g., cinnamon, red pepper flakes, ground pepper, thyme
> Small votive candle

Take two matching drinking glasses (8 – 16 oz size) and turn them upside down. Balance the Pyrex® pan on the two glasses. Fill the pan about halfway up with oil, and sprinkle spices (any one of those mentioned will do) so that most of the surface is covered.

Light the candle and slide it between the two glasses, so that the flame is about 2" from the bottom of the pan. Don't let the flame touch the glass.

Very quickly you will see the spices moving. An empty circle will appear directly above the candle, showing how the warmed oil (closest to the flame) is rising up and pushing the spices away. After a little while you will be able to see the flakes falling back down into the oil. They are actually being carried back down as cooler oil from the top sinks and the warmer oil continues to rise up.

If you are unwilling to use such a large quantity of oil, you can do the experiment with plain tap water and spices. The effect is the same, but not quite so visually dramatic. Follow the instructions above, substituting water for oil. Choose a spice that floats until it is waterlogged, then starts to sink. Red pepper flakes work well for this. After a minute or two you will see the flakes begin to sink, except in the center - over the flame they will start to go up.

This process of convection happens everywhere, from the pot on your kitchen stove to cloud formations in the sky to the vast stretches of open ocean. It's important to understand the take-home message – this process is essentially the same under all conditions. When heated, molecules move faster, and so they take up more space, and therefore are less dense than their cooler neighbors.

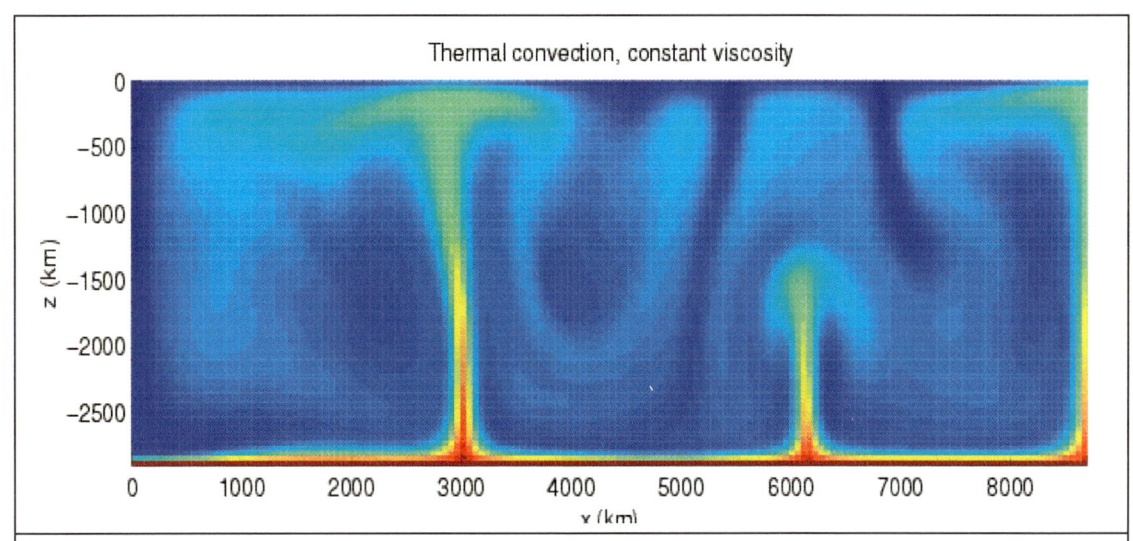

Convection way underground

This figure is a snapshot of one time-step in a model of the Earth's mantle convection. Colors closer to red are hot areas and colors closer to blue are cold areas. In this figure, heat received at the **core-mantle boundary** results in thermal expansion of the material at the bottom of the model, reducing its density and causing it to send plumes of hot material upwards. Likewise, cooling of material at the surface results in its sinking.

Image courtesy of **Harroschmeling** at **de.wikipedia**; www.commons.wikimedia.org/wiki/File:Convection-snapshot.gif

CHEMISTRY

All **matter** is made of **atoms**.

Atoms consist of three basic parts: Protons and neutrons, which are found in the center, or **nucleus**, of each atom, and **electrons**, which whirl around the nucleus. There are also sub-atomic particles which make up the protons, neutrons & electrons, but we will not go into that here. A brief explanation of The Standard Model of nuclear physics is presented in the Astronomy section. *Why astronomy? You'll see...*

A proton has a single positive electrical charge. An electron has a single negative electrical charge and a neutron has no electrical charge. In an electrically neutral atom, the number of protons and electrons are equal, thus the charges cancel each other out. The image here is a stylized version of what school children typically see in their textbooks. Protons and neutrons are clustered together in a nucleus with electrons whizzing around them. It is a reasonably efficient way to illustrate on a two-dimensional page what an atom looks like, but in reality the structure is much more complicated. Electrons are not really points, like little tiny ping pong balls orbiting around billiard balls. Rather, they are diffuse negative electrical charges that exist in a cloud around the positive energy in the atom's center. These "electron clouds" form specific, three-dimensional configurations according to laws of physics that are

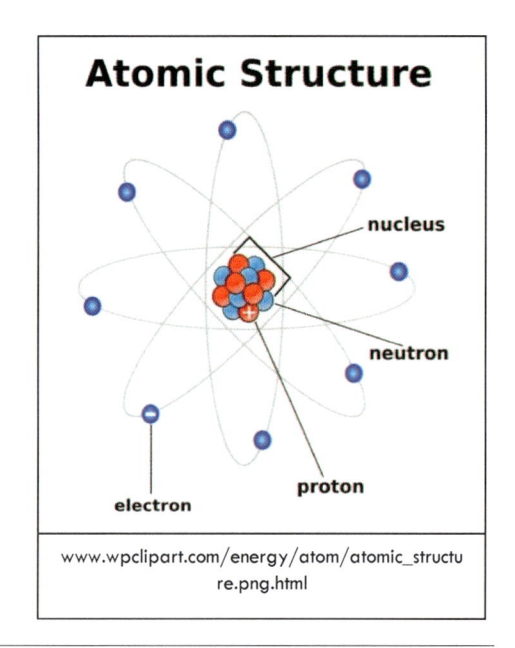

Atomic Structure

www.wpclipart.com/energy/atom/atomic_structure.png.html

beyond the scope of this book. In high school kids will learn about electron orbitals and the mathematical wave functions that govern their possible locations. But, this stylized illustration is not a bad way to begin to conceptualize atomic structure.

Elements are materials made of just one type of atom. For example, gold (Au) is a metal made entirely of gold atoms. Helium (He) is a gas made entirely of helium atoms. The way in which the individual atoms hold onto each other is the reason behind many of the physical characteristics we associate with the elements. For example, gold shines because the 3-dimensional structure formed by its atoms in a molecular lattice reflects light in the visible spectrum, which our eyes then see; hence we say that gold shines.

Titanium (Ti, atomic number 22) is a metal found commonly on Earth, but it is always bonded to other elements in Nature.

Various chemical purification processes have been developed and titanium is now used in a variety of applications, such as, in the fabrication of many metal tools, in cell phone components and in orthopedic implants.

Titanium dioxide, TiO_2 is a very bright, white powder used ubiquitously in the manufacture of paints and pigments, and, when can even be applied to skin as a sunscreen. Images courtesy of Wikipedia www.en.wikipedia.org/wiki/Titanium and www.commons.wikimedia.org/wiki/File:Titanium-dioxide-sample.jpg

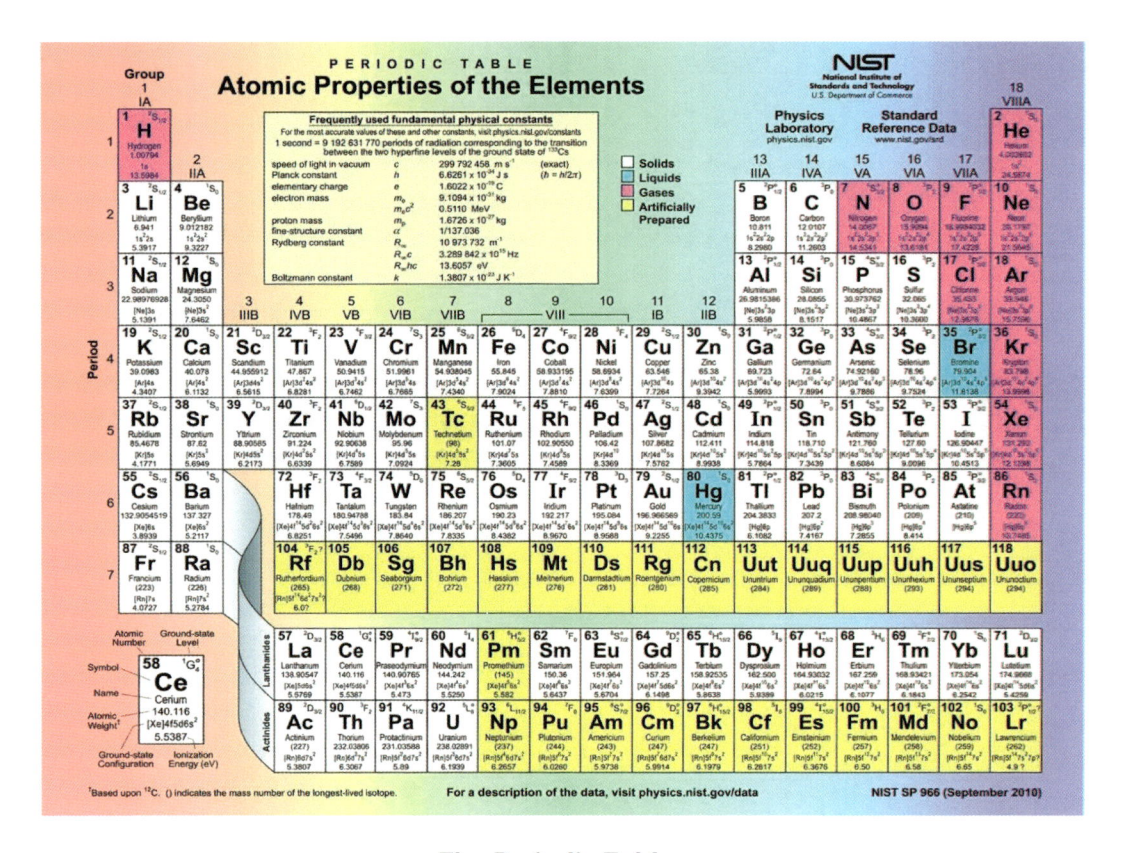

The Periodic Table

courtesy of R.A. Dragoset, A. Musgrove, C.W. Clark, and W.C. Martin — NIST, Physical Measurement Laboratory
www.commons.wikimedia.org/wiki/File:Periodic_Table_-_Atomic_Properties_of_the_Elements.png

Each element is placed in the Table by its **atomic number**, which is simply equal to the number of protons in its nucleus. There are no missing gaps or doubles in the periodic table. Every element fits sequentially with its neighbors. Hydrogen, atomic number 1, has one proton. Helium, atomic number 2, has two protons. Lithium, atomic number 3, has three protons, and so on. Both a single proton and a single neutron each have a mass defined as one **unified atomic mass unit, u**. Elements that have an equal number of protons and neutrons, have an atomic weight that is double the atomic number. However some atoms have an atomic weight that is more than twice the atomic number, indicating that the nucleus contains more neutrons than protons. For example, look at the table below:

Atomic Number	Element	Atomic Mass	# of Protons	# of Neutrons
16	Sulfur	32	16	16
17	Chlorine	35 and 37*	17	18 and 20*
18	Argon	40	18	22
19	Potassium	39 and 41*	19	20 and 22*
20	Calcium	40	20	20
21	Scandium	45	21	24
22	Titanium	46, 47, 48, 49, 50*	22	24, 25, 26, 27, 28*

What is going on here?!

Many elements, including those marked with an * here, exist in different isotopic forms. **Different isotopes of the same element simply have a different number of neutrons in their nucleus.** Note that the periodic table is built around Atomic Number, that is, the number of protons in the nucleus, and that follows a perfect linear progression. However, the number of neutrons can vary a bit, and in these cases, the nuclei of the elements do not have a strong preference for an exact number of neutrons. In the case of chlorine, for example, about 75% of the chlorine atoms on Earth have 18 neutrons, for an Atomic Mass of 35, but 25% of the chlorine atoms have 20 neutrons, and these have an Atomic Mass of 37. In the case of titanium, about 74% of this element has 26 neutrons, creating an atomic mass of 48, but the other four isotopes are about equally represented. Most charts of the periodic table will show an *average atomic mass*, when the relative abundance of all the isotopes of an element are averaged out.

Molecules

Molecules are combinations of atoms. When atoms of the same or different elements come together under the correct circumstances they combine. A molecule of two oxygen atoms stuck together, O_2, is the predominant form of oxygen in the air. Water is just the combination of one atom of oxygen and two atoms of hydrogen that have come together to form a molecule of H_2O.

A glucose molecule is written chemically as $C_6H_{12}O_6$, meaning it is made of 6 atoms of carbon, 12 atoms of hydrogen, and 6 atoms of oxygen, all bound together in a specific three-dimensional arrangement to form a single molecule of glucose.

Fructose (also known as fruit sugar) is likewise composed of 6 atoms of carbon, 12 atoms of hydrogen, and 6 atoms of oxygen, and can be written as the formula $C_6H_{12}O_6$, but the fructose molecule is arranged in a slightly different three-dimensional structure than those of glucose, and so the properties of these two molecules are slightly different as well.

Everything on Earth is made of atoms and molecules – in other words – chemicals. At the most basic level, all matter can be described in terms of the elements from which it is composed.

> ## Everyday Knowledge – Sugar
>
> Sucrose, or basic table sugar, is created by the joining of one molecule of glucose to one molecule of fructose. Glucose and fructose each have six atoms of carbon, twelve atoms of hydrogen, and six atoms of oxygen, bonded together in a particular arrangement. When a molecule of glucose and a molecule of fructose bond together, a molecule of sucrose is created. Sucrose is called a disaccharide, because it is made up of two (hence the prefix di-) sugar molecules. This is illustrated in the diagram below.

More examples:

- Table salt is sodium chloride, NaCl, one atom of sodium joined to one atom of chlorine. The molecules of NaCl connect with each other to form a lattice structure, which in turn, makes salt crystals. The bars in the illustration represent bonds of energy binding each atom to its neighbor.

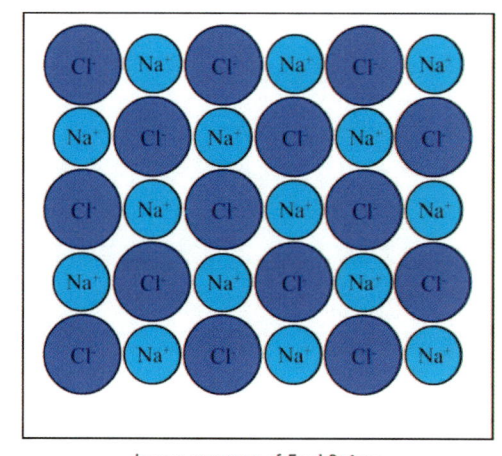

Image courtesy of Eyal Bairey
www.commons.wikimedia.org/wiki/File:NaCl_crystal_structure.png

- Rust is iron oxide, or FeO_2, two atoms of oxygen joined to one atom of iron.

- Baking soda is sodium bicarbonate, $NaHCO_3$, one atom of sodium, one atom of hydrogen, one atom of carbon, and three atoms of oxygen.

- Diamonds are pure carbon, C. These atoms are joined together in a perfect crystal lattice that gives diamonds their clarity and hardness. Coal (graphite) is also mostly pure carbon (with some impurities), but it is arranged differently at the molecular level. Whereas diamond's carbon atoms form a three-dimensional lattice, the carbon atoms in graphite form in two dimensional sheets, which are then stacked on top of each other. The result is a very different product, even though the atomic composition is very similar. Other forms of the element carbon are illustrated here.

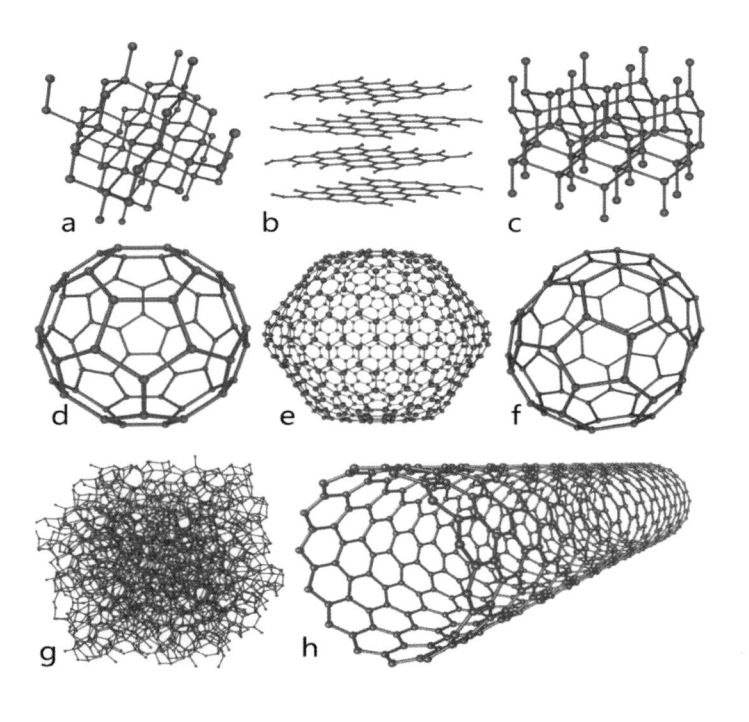

A = Diamond
B = Graphite
C = Lonsdaleite, a type of carbon molecule that forms when **meteorites** containing **graphite** strike the Earth.
D = Buckminsterfullerene
E = Fullerene
F = Fullerene
G = Coal
H = Carbon nanotube

Image courtesy of Michael Ströck
www.commons.wikimedia.org/wiki/File:Eight_Allotropes_of_Carbon.png

- All sugars, starches and fats that make up the foods we eat everyday are combinations of carbon, oxygen, hydrogen. Add a dash of nitrogen in the right places and you get protein.
- A bacterial cell (for example, *E. coli*, the kind that live in everyone's intestines) is made up of 50% carbon, 20% oxygen, 14% nitrogen, 8% hydrogen, 3% phosphorous, and 1% or less of several other elements.

- The human body is about 65% oxygen; 10% hydrogen; 18% carbon and 3% nitrogen. The other 4% of a human body is composed of small amounts of several other elements.

Everyday Knowledge – Caveat Emptor

Think about this:

Would you let your kids drink something that was fortified with Vitamin C? Of course you would – that sounds healthy. But what about something that listed an ingredient called

(5R)-((1S)-1,2-dihydroxyethyl)-3,4-dihydroxyfuran-2(5H)-one ?

Its chemical composition is six carbon atoms, five hydrogen atoms, and six oxygen atoms, or $C_6H_5O_6$. It also goes by the name "ascorbic acid", or Vitamin C.

The scientific name sounds really complicated, but this naming system simply allows chemists to describe the particular orientation of each atom in the molecule.

In fact, simple fructose, the sugar found naturally in apples and pears and grapes, and all other fruits, has the official chemical 1,3,4,5,6-Pentahydroxyhex-2-one.

That's why marketing people write "fruit sugar" on the ingredient label!

Ions

An atom that has a positive or negative electrical charge is called an ion. The designation of + and − indicates the electrical charge of that ion. As described at the beginning of this chapter, all protons carry a single positive electrical charge, and all electrons carry a single negative electrical charge. (Neutrons have no electrical charge). Neutral atoms have an equal number of protons and electrons and so their electrical charge cancels out to zero. Positive ions are missing one or more electrons, and would like to grab electron(s) from wherever they can find one to balance out their protons' positive charges. Negative ions have one or more extra electrons whirling around their nucleus, and they are willing to get rid of that extra negativity. Opposites attract. Positive ions like to bond with, or at least share the electrons of, negative ions, and vice versa. Molecules like NaCl exist because the chlorine atoms "like" being in close proximity to the sodium atoms. While these do not actually trade electrons, they both benefit by the chlorine atoms' sharing their electronegativity with the sodium atoms.

Everyday Experiment
Static Electricity

Take a balloon, or a polyester cloth of some sort, and run it over your hair. The strands of hair pick up electrons from the balloon (or cloth). Now, since each individual hair is covered with these extra electrons, each strand is negatively charged. Negative charges repel each other and so each strand of hair tries to get as far away from each other as possible, and the result is hair that "stands up" on its own.

Everyday Knowledge
Static Electricity

Everyone is familiar with getting a shock when you touch a piece of metal on a dry winter day, or of hair that flies away after being brushed or rubbed with a cloth or a balloon. Why does this happen?

Many materials will lose electrons to passing objects. If you walk over a carpet, your body actually collects some electrons from the surface of the carpet fibers. Your body is now "negatively charged", but things prefer to be neutral. The next thing (or person) you touch will be the recipient of those extra electrons. The passing of them creates a spark of electricity, specifically the transfer of electrons. This affect is much more pronounced during the winter because the ambient air is drier in the winter, and more humid in the summer. Moisture in the air itself will absorb these extra electrons generated and so they will disperse without you really noticing. However, when the ambient air is very dry, there is no place for the electrons to go, until you physically touch another object.

Static electricity is called by this name because static means in-place. The electrons you collect walking across a carpet do not flow anywhere until you touch a doorknob or something else that you can transfer these extra electrons to. Static is different from current, which indicates a flow of electrons.

Electricity happens when an atom or molecule loses an electron, and this negative charge travels through some material, displacing more electrons from more atoms, and setting off a cascade of more electrons all moving in the same direction. Some materials, for example the element copper, provide particularly good "roads" for this type of electron travel. This is why electrical wires are often made of copper. Electrons can easily travel from one atom of copper to the next, like dominoes. Other substances have a higher **resistance** to electron movement. The transmission of electrons, or negative electrical charges, is what electricity is.

Chemical reactions take place when atoms or molecules combine with or break apart from each other. During a chemical reaction, atoms share or transfer their electrons among each other. Molecules can be broken down to their component atoms and reconfigured with atoms from another molecule. **No atoms can ever be lost or changed into another atom because of a chemical reaction**, but they can be shuffled and re-sorted to form different **molecules.**

There are different ways that atoms bond with other atoms to create molecules, the main ones being:

Ionic

Covalent

Metallic

Hydrogen

Ionic bonds occur between two atoms that have very different **electronegativity**. Even though all atoms are neutral, that is, they have equal numbers of positively-charged protons and negatively-charged electrons that balance each other out, some atoms "hold onto" their electrons much more tightly, while others "hold onto" their electrons much more loosely. Atoms with higher electronegativity tend to attract negatively charged electrons from other atoms; those with lower electronegativity tend to give up their own electrons more easily to other atoms. This relative attraction of the outermost (a.k.a. valence) electrons in a given atom is called its electronegativity. For example, chlorine (Cl) normally has a "vacancy" in its outer electron orbital that it would like to fill. Another atom, let's say, sodium (Na) has an electron that it can only weakly hold on to, as it is located in an orbital that is too far away from the nucleus to feel very loved. When these two atoms come together, that negative charge from the sodium jumps into the available space in the chlorine's orbital. In doing so, the sodium atom now becomes a positively charged sodium ion (Na^+) because it now has only ten electrons balancing its eleven protons and the chlorine atom now becomes a negatively charged chlorine ion (Cl^-) because it now has 18 electrons and only 17 protons. Now that they have opposite charges, and opposites attract, the ions can form an ionic bond and a three dimensional lattice, as in the picture above.

Everyday Experiment –
The Famous Kitchen Sink Volcano

A simple, safe, cheap and fun chemical reaction to do with your kids is to mix regular household vinegar with baking soda to create an explosion in the kitchen sink. This clearly illustrates the concept of a chemical reaction. With a little explanation as to what's really happening at a molecular level, it can go a long way towards helping young kids "get" chemistry.

Begin by placing about ¼ cup of baking soda in a large glass jar, about 1 or 1.5 cup size. For easy clean-up, place the jar in the sink. Pour about ½ cup of vinegar into a small bottle or measuring cup and slowly pour on top of the baking soda. Almost immediately the two will react and start a bubbly explosion.

Baking Soda, or sodium bicarbonate, can be written in scientific form as **NaHCO$_3$**. It is made up of one sodium atom, one hydrogen atom, one carbon atom, and three oxygen atoms, arranged in a particular shape.

Plain old white vinegar from the grocery store is a solution of 5% acetic acid in water. Acetic acid can be written in scientific form as **CH$_3$COOH**. The baking soda is a solid, and so the sodium, carbon, and oxygen atoms that it is made of are already pretty content to be sitting in this particular molecular arrangement. The acetic acid molecule, however, is already mixed up in water, and so the atoms are constantly moving around in this solution. The arrow pointing in both directions indicates that this reaction is constantly going both ways. This can be written out scientifically as

$$CH_3COOH + H_2O \longleftrightarrow H^+ + CH_3COO^- + H^+ + OH^-$$

As vinegar is poured over the baking soda, baking soda dissolves into sodium (Na$^+$) and bicarbonate ions (HCO$_3^-$)

The vinegar reacts with the baking soda to form two new chemicals: sodium acetate, **NaC$_2$H$_3$O$_2$** and carbonic acid, **H$_2$CO$_3$**.

$$H^+ + CH_3COO^- + H^+ + OH^- + Na^+ + HCO_3^- \longleftrightarrow NaC_2H_3O_2 + H_2CO_3 + H_2O$$

The carbonic acid then immediately decomposes into carbon dioxide gas and water:

$$H_2CO_3 \longrightarrow H_2O + CO_2 \quad \text{(note this arrow only goes in one direction)}$$

It's this carbon dioxide gas that you see bubbling and foaming as soon as you mix baking soda and vinegar together. The remaining sodium acetate, or **NaC$_2$H$_3$O$_2$** in water, **H$_2$O** can just be rinsed down the sink!

Covalent Bonds result when two (or more) atoms of similar electronegativity share electrons with each other. In doing so, both atoms become more stable ("happier") than they were alone. Covalent bonds are the dominant force in organic (carbon-containing) chemistry. The carbon atom itself is uniquely qualified to participate in a variety of sharing configurations, both with other carbon atoms and with many other atoms as well. This is because carbon's outermost electron orbital is naturally half full (or half empty, if you are that kind of person). Carbon loves to bond with other atoms in order to feel that its outer orbitals are satisfied. Each "bond" refers to a shared pair of electrons, one from each of the participating atoms. Sometimes a single bond is formed, under different conditions two pairs of electrons are shared, resulting in a double bond, and occasionally even a triple bond can be formed.

This carbon to carbon bonding is essential for life on Earth (see the Life Sciences chapter). The chemical composition of various sugars and other foods were mentioned above, all of which contain carbon. In addition, this desire of carbon atoms to bond with each other can result in **polymerization**, which is the propagation of bonds between atoms that results in a gigantic molecule of repeating units. Polyester

A molecule of triglyceride, a tri-ester, found in a linseed oil derived of **linoleic acid, alpha-linolenic acid,** and **oleic acid.** Each angle represents a carbon atom.

Image courtesy of Ju, via www.en.wikipedia.org/wiki/Ester#Structure_and_bonding

(yes, the fabric) is simply a *polymer* created by linking a string of *esters* (a particular configuration of a carbon, oxygen and hydrogen containing molecule) into a new molecular configuration.

Metallic Bonds

In ionic and covalent bonds the sharing of electrons is localized between two atoms, but in metals the cloud of electrons is delocalized, meaning that the negative charge is shared by many, many atoms simultaneously. It is this delocalized sharing that gives metals their characteristic properties of strength, durability, high melting points, luster and conductivity. Some non-metals, like the graphene form of carbon, can also form metallic bonds. Mercury (H_g) is a metal (the only metal that exists as a liquid at room temperature), and it forms covalent bonds. However, in general metallic bonding is a distinctive property of metals.

Hydrogen Bonds

These are relatively weak interactions, as compared to the other three examples above, but yet they are very important in chemistry. Hydrogen atoms are often covalently bonded to other atoms. When the other atom is one with a high electronegativity (as described above, this means an atom that "likes" to accept electrons from other atoms) that atom exerts a very strong pull on the hydrogen's lone electron. That leaves the hydrogen nucleus (a single positively charged proton) rather exposed. In a solution with lots of hydrogen nuclei so exposed, these tend to get close to the electrons of neighboring molecules and hence a loose network of hydrogen bonded molecules is formed.

In water based (aqueous) solutions, hydrogen bonding is extremely important. Most chemical reactions take place in solution, that is, when one substance is dissolved in another substance, called a solvent. Many, many chemical reactions are based on the dissolving of molecules in water, as the water molecule, H_2O, is an excellent host for reactions to take place in. This is true on every scale. Adding water while cooking enables different food molecules to interact and thereby change their taste and texture. Stomach acids help you to digest food by providing an acidic, aqueous solution in which food molecules get broken down and recombined to make other molecules that are easier for your body to use. Blood is an aqueous solution that carries nutrients and waste products, along with oxygen, to all parts of an organism's body. Every body of water such as lakes and rivers, are, at the molecular level, aqueous solutions in which myriad chemical reactions take place.

Perhaps most fundamentally important of all is the oceans. Everyone knows that there is salt (NaCl and other salts too) in ocean water, but the oceans are actually a vast, dynamic chemical solution. Carbon dioxide in the atmosphere, calcium carbonate dissolving from the shells of dead sea creatures, organic (carbon-containing) molecules from all the living plants and creatures who reside there all are in constant, dynamic motion, reacting with each other to break and re-build chemical bonds, hence creating different chemical mixes every minute of every day and have done so for billions of years. There are many more ingredients too: vents and volcanoes deep under the sea spew out plumes of chemicals that scientists are just beginning to learn about. Pollution and runoff from land ends up in oceans as well.

Not everything can be dissolved in water. The old saying about oil and water not mixing is as true as ever. That's why salad dressings need to be shaken. They are made of oil, which cannot be molecularly mixed with water, and most of the other stuff is vinegar (which is an aqueous acidic solution). Oil molecules (whether you are talking about olive oil or motor oil) are made of chains of atoms (carbon, hydrogen, oxygen) but these atoms interact with each other in such a way that they repel H_2O molecules. Oils prefer to adhere closely to other. They can certainly be mixed up (by a spoon or by being physically shaken together) but, left alone, Nature will take over and these water and oil based molecules will separate into two distinct layers.

Two examples of oil and water

Olive Oil in water

Image courtesy of
commons.wikimedia.org/wiki/
File:Oil_in_water.jpg

Location of Oil Slick on water

Image of oil slick in the Gulf of Mexico

Image courtesy of NASA at
www.earthobservatory.nasa.gov/NaturalHazards/view.php?id=43768&eocn=image&eoci=nh_viewall

Everyday Knowledge
Food

A long time ago food scientists figured out a way to take advantage of Nature's basic designs and make foods in which oil and water could stay mixed up. How did they do this?

Ingredients called emulsifiers are often added to processed food. These are molecules that are two-faced. They have hydrophilic (water –liking) sites and hydrophobic (water-hating) sites. The hydrophilic sites on the emulsifier molecule are attracted to the aqueous molecules around them, and the hydrophobic sites are attracted to the oil-based molecules. Since the emulsifier is a single molecule itself, it allows molecular enemies to be brought together and to remain smoothly integrated.

Lecithin is a very common such ingredient. Look for this on the ingredient labels on your favorite chocolate!

Everyday Experiment
Food

Get two paper plates. Take a tablespoon of oil (canola, vegetable or olive will do), pour it onto one of the plates. Spread the oil around with a paper towel. Now take a teaspoon of water and sprinkle this over the oiled plate. Sprinkle another teaspoon of water over the clean plate.

What happens? The water on the clean plate will spread out, but on the oily plate the water should coalesce into tight, rounded droplets. This is because the water molecules are repelled by the hydrophobic oil, and try to stay together as much as possible.

Everyday Experiment - Clothing

Why are certain fabrics used for casual clothing, and other fabrics used for athletic attire? The answer lies in their relative hydrophilicity or hydrophobicity of the chemicals that they are made of.

Cotton and silk are natural substances. Both of these hydrophilic (water loving) materials have molecular structures that encourage the absorption of water molecule into the fabric itself.

Polyester fleece, which many modern clothing products are made of, is a hydrophobic (water hating) material which actually repels water droplets at the molecular level. Water stays on the surface of fleece, making it water-repellant. This property keeps you relatively dry in a rainstorm. However, given enough water and time, water will penetrate fleece, and once that happens, the water there attracts more water.

Raincoats and other gear can be made of any number of hydrophobic materials. Rubber, nylon, polyurethane, and others will repel water and keep the wearer dry. They also trap sweat inside, so they are not very comfortable to exercise in.

GoreTex™ is the gold standard in water resistant clothing. This material (and others made with similar functionality) is made of molecules that chemically repel water on the outside from getting in, but are perforated with extremely tiny holes so that water generated on the inside (like sweat) can escape, keeping the wearer dry on the inside.

Take a cotton T-shirt (check the label!) dunk it under water for a few seconds,, and the fabric will become completely soaked. Do the same thing with a raincoat or a fleece scarf. You will see the water run off, leaving the fabric dry. Over time water molecules can "wet" fleece, but it takes a while. You can run from the house to the car in most fleece jackets and stay quite dry, but if you stand in a hard rain for several minutes, the fabric will eventually absorb the water.

Catalysts

Sometimes atoms need a push to get together. Molecular bonds will form only if the net result is a lower energy state for the component parts. So using the sugar example from before, the collective energy in the bonds of sucrose is less than the collective energy in the bonds of the individual fructose and glucose molecules. However, some energy is required to initiate the binding of these two molecules. This is called the **activation energy** of the reaction. This diagram shows the increase in energy required to get through the transition state and eventually achieve the lower energy state.

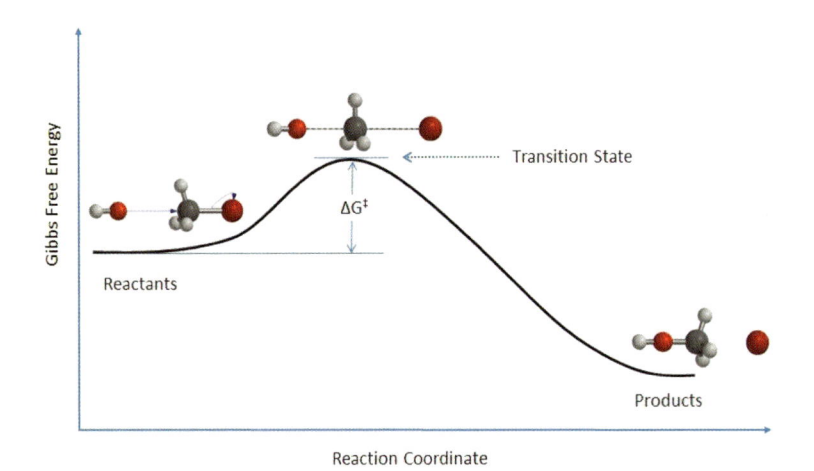

Reaction: $HO^- + CH_3Br \rightarrow [HO\text{---}CH_3\text{---}Br]^\ddagger \rightarrow CH_3OH + Br^-$

Image courtesy of www.en.wikipedia.org/wiki/Transition_state_theory

Some reactions require a special chemical helper called a **catalyst** to get the reactants "over the hump" of the transition state and enable reaction to take place at all. Catalysts are found everywhere. In Nature they control innumerable functions of cells. Engineers have created thousands of chemicals that act as catalysts in industrial processes that allow the creation of new molecules with desirable characteristics that were not found in Nature. Catalysts, however, never participate in the reactions they enable - they serve as disinterested parties. Think about a typical high school dance: A boy and a girl may want to dance with each other, but are too shy to actually speak. The activation energy of their making contact with each other is simply too great for the two interested parties to overcome. However, enter a friend, a catalyst, who brings the two parties together by starting a conversation about something of mutual interest. Once the original boy and girl are deep in conversation, the friend will leave, completely unchanged by the interaction.

ASTRONOMY

In school, kids learn about our own Solar System – the sun and planets and their satellites. They will learn how our Earth rotates around its own axis and revolves around the Sun. They will learn basic facts like how far away these different bodies are from each other, and why it is colder in winter and warmer in summer. But a good way to truly understand the Solar System is to begin the same way it (and everything else) began:

About 13.7 billion years ago Something happened. This "Something" is often referred to as the "Big Bang", which was the beginning of all matter and energy and time in the universe as we know it today. It is very difficult to imagine in any accurate way, but scientific evidence suggests that there was a unique, unimaginably high-energy singularity which released its contents in all directions. This was the beginning of the Universe. Everything originated in that initial burst.

This theory has been constructed based upon decades of research in astronomy and physics. In order to learn about the vastness of the universe, scientists must study the smallest of things. Everyone knows that stuff is made of atoms, but what are atoms made of? Atoms are made of protons, neutrons and electrons, but what are those made of? Well, as far as we can see, electrons are just electrons, and a single electron is a single unit of negative charge. Protons and neutrons, however, are made of elementary particles called **quarks**. Actually two "up" quarks and one "down" quark makes up a proton, and two down quarks and one up quark makes a neutron and these quarks are held together by **gluons**. These particles can be quantified in terms of their energy, and that is why the **E = mc²** equation is so important... but that's probably all the detail we need to go into in this book.

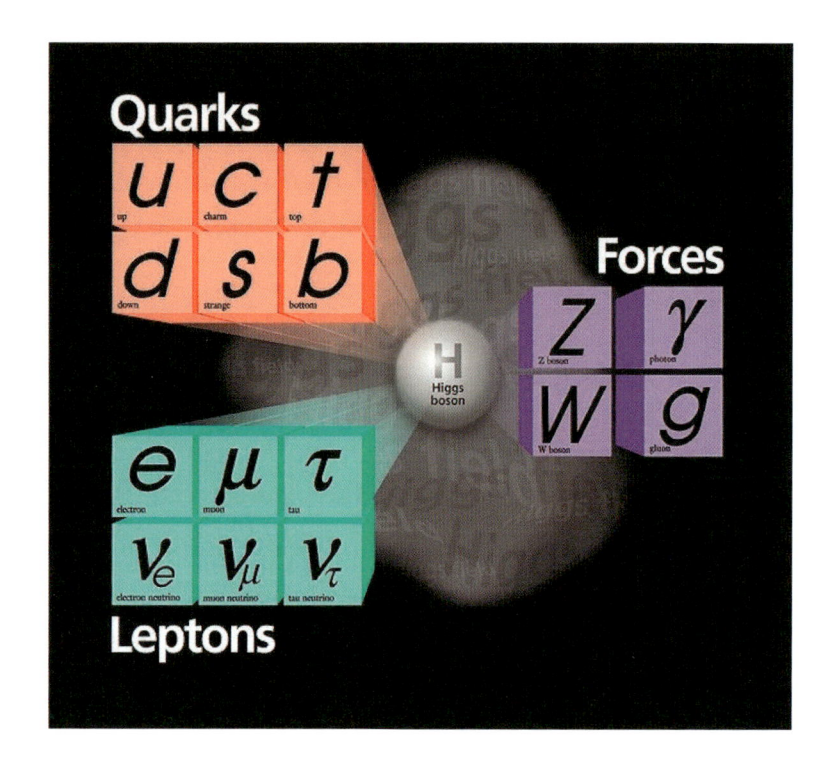

The Standard Model of Elementary Particles

Image courtesy of Fermi National Accelerator Laboratory (Fermi Lab) via www.commons.wikimedia.org/wiki/File:Standard_Model_From_Fermi_Lab.jpg

It is well accepted as fact that the Universe is expanding, that is has always been expanding, and continues to do so today. By extrapolating backwards, physicists have calculated that for the first ten thousandth (10^{-5}) of a second after the Big Bang all that existed were elementary particles (the above-mentioned quarks, electrons, *et. al.*) and massive quantities of energy. As the volume of all this stuff continued to expand, it cooled.

History of the Universe

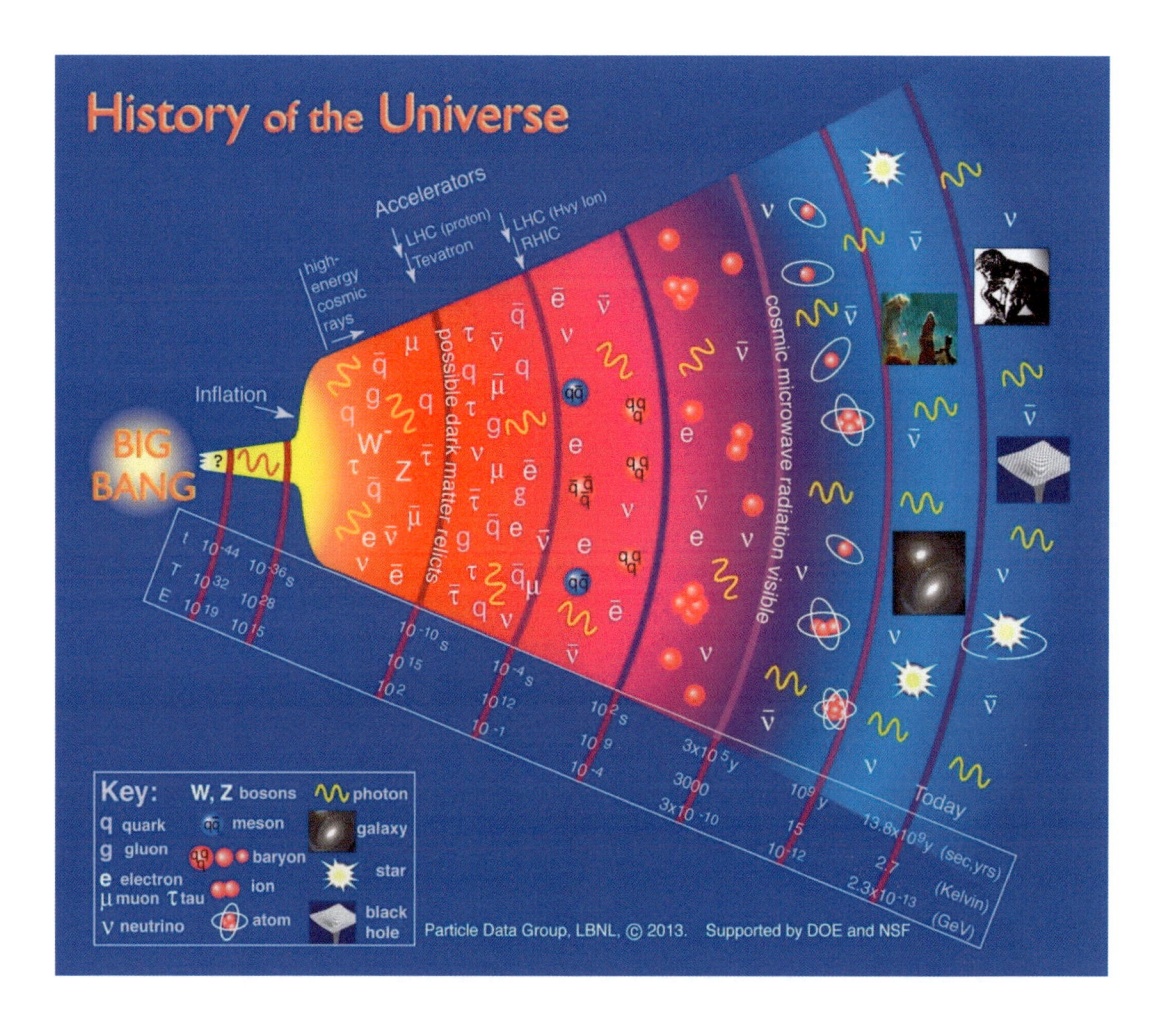

Look at the image above and notice that between one ten thousandth (10^{-5}) of a second and about 100 (10^2) seconds after the Big Bang, the temperature of the Universe dropped by 3 orders of magnitude, from 10^{12} to 10^9 degrees Kelvin. As the particles' temperatures lowered (and therefore the pressure decreased) some of them were able to stick together to form atomic nuclei of hydrogen.

In addition to hydrogen nuclei (remember - the nucleus of a hydrogen atom is simply one proton) some protons fused together with neutrons to form nuclei of deuterium, which is a heavier form of hydrogen (regular hydrogen doesn't have a neutron in its nucleus). A fraction of these deuterium atoms crashed so forcefully into each other that helium nuclei formed (2 protons + 2 neutrons).

This state of high energy subatomic particles and small atomic nuclei whizzing around continued for about a half a million years. During that time the Universe and its contents continued to expand. Since the volume increased (**PV** ∝ **T**) the pressure decreased, which caused a further decrease in temperature. This cooling allowed more stuff to stick together. Soon, electrons joined with the nuclei described above to form the first **atoms** of hydrogen, deuterium and helium. The stage was set for the next big event…the birth of stars.

Star forming in the 30 Doradus Nebulla, a region in the Large Magellanic Cloud

Image courtesy of NASA, ESA, and F. Paresce (INAF-IASF, Bologna, Italy), R. O'Connell (University of Virginia, Charlottesville), and the Wide Field Camera 3 Science Oversight Committee
www.nasa.gov/mission_pages/hubble/science/hst_img_festive_r136.html

Image courtesy of NASA.gov **www.nasa.gov/sites/default/files/heic1406a.jpg**

With NASA's Hubble Space Telescope, astronomers have captured infrared-light images of a churning region of star birth 6,400 light-years away. Massive newborn stars near the center of the nebula (and toward the right in this image) are blasting away at dust within the nebula. The ultraviolet light emitted by these bright stars helps shape the dust into giant pillars.

STARS

We are all made of stardust. In fact, everything on Earth originated in stars. As magical an idea as that is, there really is some hard science behind it! As the universal expansion continued after the Big Bang, in some areas fantastically large clouds of (mostly) hydrogen atoms started to form. Such a huge cloud of gas gets pulled inward by its own gravity. This increases the density at the center of the cloud, which increases the pressure, and an increase in pressure will always cause an increase in temperature. In the case of these clouds, the core temperature reaches at least 10 million degrees Kelvin. The intense pressure and temperature inside these gas clouds led to the **fusion** of atomic nuclei, eventually creating the nuclei of larger elements.

Stars have a lifespan with a beginning, middle, and end. Over millions of years the composition of gases in any star will change. Stars spend about 90% of their life in the **Main Sequence Phase**, during which they fuse hydrogen into helium, and create energy from this nuclear fusion reaction. When a star's hydrogen runs out, the star is predominantly composed of helium. Three helium (He) atoms can fuse together to create larger atoms of carbon (C), which has six protons and six neutrons in its nucleus. Eventually (after millions of years) the star collapses onto itself. Again, this collapse causes an increase in the density of the star.

> Stars are basically balls of burning gas. But don't confuse this with the kind of burning we have here on Earth. On Earth, a fire is fueled by oxygen, and there is no free oxygen in outer space. At the center of a star, the pressure is so great and the temperature so hot that hydrogen atoms are changed into helium atoms through the process of **nuclear fusion**. This process emits enormous quantities of energy, and this released energy is the source of the brightness of stars.

If a star is large enough, some of the carbon atoms are further fused into even heavier elements. Eventually, in the largest stars, iron (Fe) nuclei are formed. At this point, the iron nuclei absorb the remaining energy until the moment when it all explodes. This is called a **Supernova** explosion. The heat of a supernova explosion fuses more protons and neutrons together, thus creating atomic nuclei much larger than iron, and completing the creation of all naturally occurring elements in the Periodic Table. The explosion also causes all these atoms to be then flung across the cosmos. ***They form the building blocks of everything else in the Universe.***

> After this type of a Supernova explosion, what is left of the original star is called a **neutron star.** These regions of dense matter emit no light, and so are not visible to us on Earth. However, neutron stars do emit radio waves that astronomers' instruments can detect. When a neutron star emits its radio waves in a regular pattern of pulses, it is referred to as a **pulsar.**

The same process continues today. Astronomers have found many "stellar nurseries" where the process of star formation is happening in clouds of cosmic hydrogen. There is a continual process of creation, destruction and regeneration. Stars are formed from the intense heat and pressure inside clouds of gas. They increase in intensity until they implode, and when they do, their component gases are blown throughout the vast expanses of space. Eventually, gravitational attraction causes wisps of gases to coalesce into new clouds, and the process continues.

> The really cool take-home message here is that all the elements originated either during the Big Bang or in stars. The carbon in your body, the oxygen in the air, the chlorine in bleach, the calcium in milk, the zinc in multivitamins — all this originated inside a star in the very distant past. In other words, everything, including you, is made of stardust. That is not a fairytale, it's science. And the real story is as fascinating as any you could find in a storybook or a song.

The Periodic Table colored to show the origins of all the elements

White - Big Bang
Pink - Cosmic Rays
Yellow - Small Stars
Green - Large Stars
Blue - Supernovae
Grey - Man Made

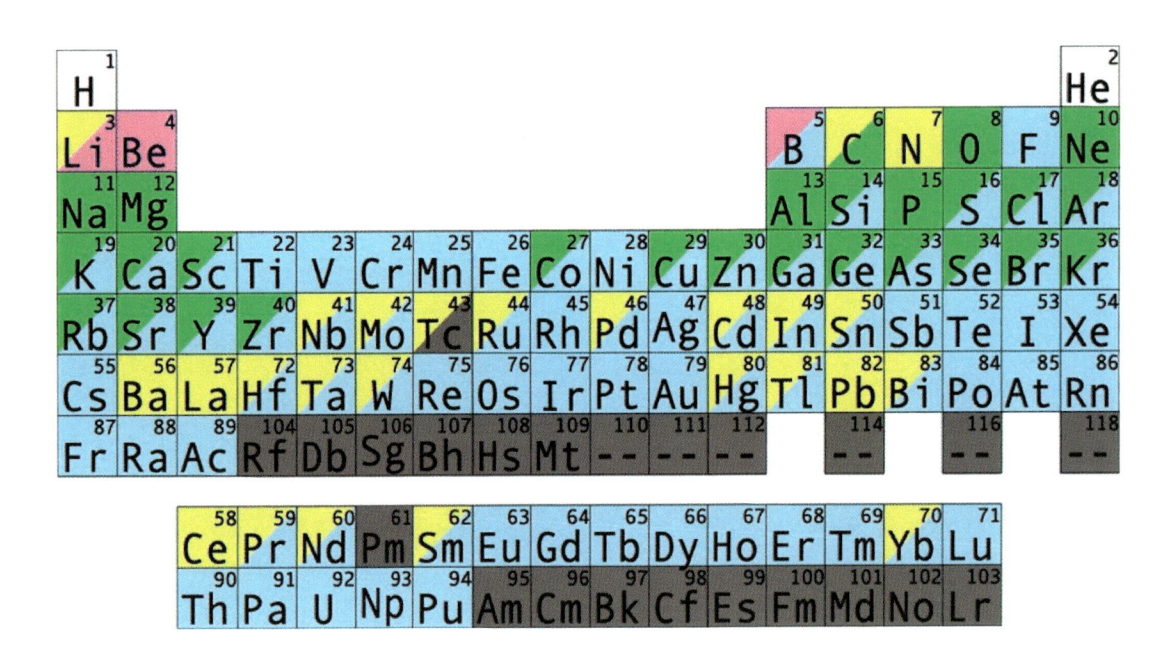

www.nasa.gov/pdf/190387main_Cosmic_Elements.pdf

GALAXIES

Galaxies are enormous clusters of stars. After the Big Bang occurred, great masses of dust and gas started coalescing into more defined groups, leaving empty spaces between these groups. More stars formed inside them, and this process of star formation happened *billions of times* within each large mass. The stars' gravitational fields held each other together. This is how galaxies formed. Astronomers estimate that there are *hundreds of billions* of galaxies in the Universe.

We live in the **Milky Way** galaxy. This is a spiral galaxy, with visible "arms" spinning out from a defined center point. Scientists estimate that our galaxy formed relatively soon after the Big Bang, dating it at about 13 billion years old.

Image courtesy of NASA
www.en.wikipedia.org/wiki/Milky_way
NASA/JPL-Caltech/ESO/R. Hurt

Our Sun is just one of a few hundred billion stars in the Milky Way. The diameter of our entire galaxy is about 100,000 **light-years**. (One light year is the distance that light can travel in one year through outer space – about 6 trillion miles, or 9.5 trillion kilometers). Our solar system lies about 25,000 light-years from the center of the galaxy, towards the outer edge, along one of its spiral arms. It takes about 225 million years for our solar system to orbit around the center of the Milky Way.

Being inside the Milky Way, we cannot get a picture of the entire galaxy. But our galaxy has a neighbor, the Andromeda Galaxy, which we can see quite well, with the proper equipment. Below are two images from NASA.gov:

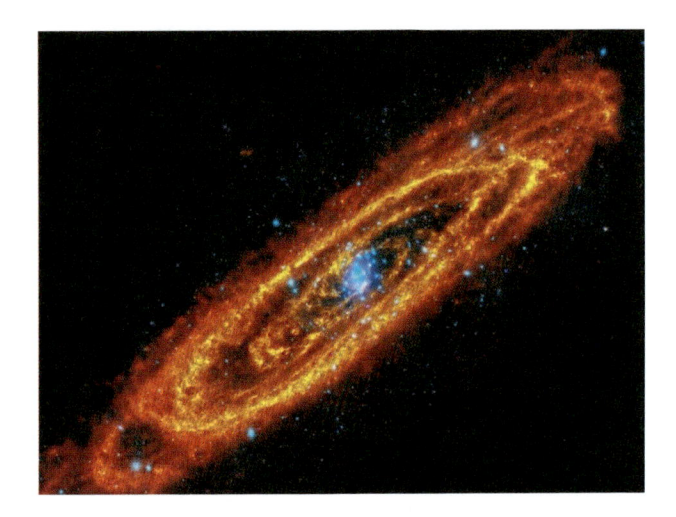

Andromeda's Once & Future Stars

This image was taken by the European Space Agency using two different telescopes, one which "sees" in the infrared spectrum and the other in the X-ray spectrum. The former shows the birth of new stars and the latter shows the radiation caused by cell death. The colors are added by scientists to help us visualize these phenomena.

Image courtesy of www.nasa.gov/multimedia/imagegallery/image_feature_1837.html

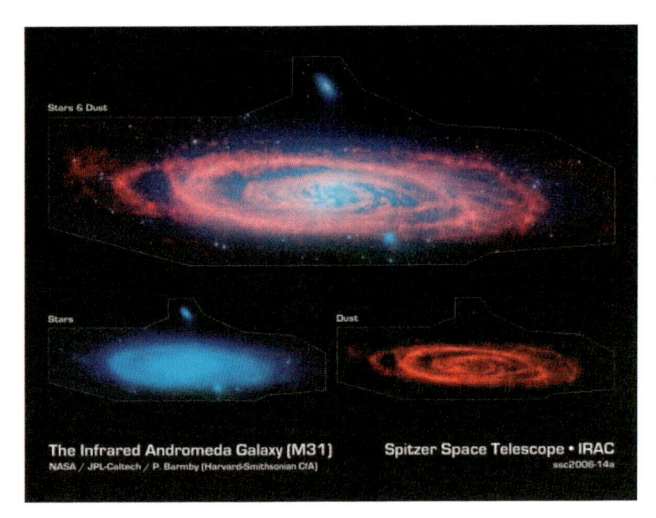

These images of Andromeda show the blue center filled with older stars while the surrounding red areas indicate regions of new star formation. This is typical of spiral galaxies, where the centers are generally populated by older stars and the edges are home to stellar nurseries. The top is a composite and the bottom two show areas of different types of radiation separated out.

Image courtesy of www.spitzer.caltech.edu/images/1630-ssc2006-14a-Andromeda-Makes-a-Splash

Everyday Activity - View the Milky Way

Parts of the Milky Way can be seen from anywhere on Earth, if the night is clear and if you happen to be in an area with little artificial light. Go outside several hours after dark, preferably on a night with no moon, and look straight up into the sky. Give your eyes a few minutes to adjust to the darkness. Large bands of stars stretching from horizon to horizon will become visible. This is our arm of the Milky Way. A telescope will enable you to see much more, but even a pair of binoculars can greatly increase the number of stars visible to anyone. If you live in or near a big city many of the stars will not be visible because of light pollution, yet very bright stars can still usually be seen. On the other hand, most cities offer planetariums and science museums where you can take your kids to learn more about astronomy, but nothing is quite as good as the real thing.

At home, check out these wonderful collections of space pictures with from the Spitzer infra-red telescope through the California Institute of technology website. Search the internet for coolcosmos.

www.Astronomy.com , the website of Astronomy magazine, also has wonderful images, online games, and informative lessons and up-to-date news on astronomical research.

For fun games & activities with astronomy themes, go to the www.nasa.gov website and go straight to the NASA Kids' Club page.

When we look up to the sky, much of the light from our neighboring stars is blocked by clouds of gas and dust swirling between Earth and the stars. These particles of dust absorb much of the visible light. However, they do not absorb much in the infrared wavelengths. What would we see if our eyes could peer through the dust?

Earth's View of The Milky Way in Infrared

This Atlas Image Mosaic was obtained as part of the 2 Micron All Sky Survey (2MASS), a joint project between the University of Massachusetts and the Infrared Processing and Analysis Center at the California Institute of Technology, funded by NASA and the National Science Foundation.

Image credited to J. Carpenter, T. H. Jarrett, & R. Hurt, November 2014.

This awesome image was taken by a telescope positioned above the Earth's own atmosphere, which absorbs much of the infrared radiation, looking towards the center of the Milky Way. It sees in infrared. Being able to eliminate the cloaking effects of our own atmosphere and of the dust particles of the Milky Way, this image gives us the most detailed view to date of what our Galaxy looks like, from Earth looking towards the center.

The Solar System

As described in the "Stars" section, stars are born in the centers of massive, swirling clouds of gas and dust. Like all stars, this is how our Sun began.

In the case of our Solar System, the rest of the gas and dust cloud continued to spin around this baby Sun, and over a few hundred million years it formed into a flattened disk shape, kind of like the way a ball of dough can be spun into a flat pizza crust. At this stage the gas cloud became a **proplyd**, which stands for proto-planetary disk. As all this stuff was spinning around the infant Sun, collisions between small clusters of matter occurred. These clusters would sometimes stick together and form larger bodies. The heavier clusters attracted other, lighter clusters to their own gravitational fields. Eventually, this whirling collection of particles formed distinct planets and moons and asteroids, all which still orbit around the central Sun, the most massive object in the Solar System. The Solar System, and the Earth itself, took shape approximately 4.567 billion years ago.

One important take home message from this is that the buildings blocks of everything on Earth today, the rocks, the water, sand, leaves on trees and fur on rabbits and our own flesh and blood were present in that original proplyd. It took many millions of years of chemical and biochemical reactions to go from the original cloud of gas and dust through the formation and maturation of the planets, but everything in the entire Solar System originated in that enormous, spinning mass of stellar gas and dust. Even the comets and asteroids that still occasionally bombard our planet were formed from the same original ingredients.

We can't watch our own planet being formed, but scientists are looking at the formation of exoplanets in other parts of the universe. This image shows a region of intense star formation in the Great Nebula of the constellation Orion, which is visible to the unaided eye near the "belt". Insets to this mosaic show numerous proplyds. Proplyds whose disks are very close to their host star appear bright, while other proplyds whose disks are stretched further from their host star (and so contain cooler dust) appear as dark silhouettes. The study of this dust, in particular, provides insight as to how these planets are forming.

Planetary Systems Now Forming in Orion
Credit: NASA, ESA, M. Robberto (STScI/ESA), the HST Orion Treasury Project Team, & L. Ricci (ESO) and the **Hubble Space Telescope**

www.spacetelescope.org/news/heic0917/

Our Planets

Mercury - Venus - Earth - Mars - Jupiter - Saturn - Uranus - Neptune - Pluto

The first four planets are small and rocky. The four farthest from the Sun are called gas giants. Pluto, the former planet, is shown at the very end of the line to show its size relative to the others. This image shows the relative sizes of our planets, but not the relative distance from the Sun.

Since the distances between bodies in outer space are so large, it gets confusing to describe them using our common units of miles or kilometers. Scientists therefore use a unit of measurement called an "**Astronomical Unit**" which is equal to 93 million miles. If you notice from the table below, 1 AU is defined as the distance between our Earth and the Sun. This makes it easy to understand the relative sizes of all the planets' orbits.

Planet	Distance from the Sun *	Diameter in Miles
Mercury	36 Million Miles / 0.38 AU	3,032
Venus	67 Million Miles / 0.72 AU	7,521
Earth	93 Million Miles / 1 AU	7,926
Mars	141 Million Miles / 1.52 AU	4,217
Jupiter	484 Million Miles / 5.2 AU	88,731
Saturn	888 Million Miles / 9.54 AU	74,564
Uranus	1.78 Billion Miles / 19.2 AU	31,763
Neptune	2.78 Billion Miles / 30.1 AU	30,775

* Every planet in our solar system has an elliptical orbit, which means that it is more oval, or egg-shaped, than circular. Therefore at some times of the year the planet is closer to the sun than at other times. The distances presented here are averages over the course of each planet's year, or the length of time it takes that planet to orbit around the Sun.

Between Jupiter and Mars is the **asteroid belt** , a collection of small, rocky chunks that orbit the Sun as if they really wanted to be planets, too, but just aren't quite big enough. The largest of these objects, Ceres, is designated a **dwarf planet** (just like Pluto).

Dwarf Planet	Distance from Sun (At the closest and farthest points of orbit)	Diameter in Miles
Ceres	2.7 AU	590
Pluto	49 AU / 30 AU	1,412
Eris	98 AU / 38 AU	1,491
Makemake	53 AU / 39 AU	932
Haumea	51 AU / 35 AU	870

The Parsec

Astronomers often use another unit to measure the incredibly huge distances in space. The distance in parsecs is found using some advanced trigonometry, which we will not go into here. Suffice it to say that the word is derived from the "parallax of an arc second". When all is calculated, 1 parsec is roughly equal to:

31 trillion kilometers, or 19 trillion miles, or; 3.3 light years.

Did you have a hard time with Pluto getting "downgraded"?

Anyone born between the early 1930's and the late 1990's has childhood memories of learning about nine planets, the last one with the cutest name. This actually provides a good example of the way science changes over time when new information becomes available.

If you think the news about Pluto was hard to take, imagine the outrage in the 1530's when Nicholas Copernicus first proposed the idea that the Earth revolved around the Sun! For thousands of years, ever since humans were able to think about such things, most people thought that the Earth stood still as the Sun and stars revolved around it. This certainly made sense, given that the Sun comes up in the east every morning and sets in the west every night. But when astronomers really started to take careful measurements of the movements of the Sun and different stars that are visible only at certain times of the year, they realized that this arrangement simply could not be true. They worked hard, taking lots of measurements and doing lots of math, to come up with a different model that would fit their data.

Nicholas Copernicus was one of the first to figure out a new explanation, namely that the Earth revolves around the Sun. Many people argued that his "heliocentric" (sun-centered) model contradicted the Bible, and so could not possibly be true. Other scientifically minded observers paid dearly for contradicting the accepted dogma. But Copernicus himself was an official in the Catholic Church, and he enjoyed the respect and friendship of many influential religious leaders. His radical ideas started to spread throughout the scientific community around Europe.

Eventually this model was accepted by more and more people. As technology improved, and more information became available, some details of the

Copernican model were altered and improved upon. But his contribution was a crucial step on the path to understanding how our world works.

Such truly profound changes in the accepted wisdom of Science are called **"Paradigm Shifts"**. While Science is always adding to its collective body of knowledge and updating older theories, a true paradigm shift, such as Copernicus' heliocentric model of the solar system, entails a radically new way of explaining the world. What paradigm shifts will come to us and our children? Currently some astronomers are investigating the hypothesized existence of a "Multiverse". As incomprehensibly large as our Universe is now known to be, it may actually be just one piece of a much larger multiverse, which encompasses billions of universes...

THE MOON

People have worshipped and studied the moon for thousands of years. Since humans first recorded their thoughts, the moon has figured prominently in songs, sagas, and stories in every culture. Ancient people doubtlessly spent more time observing the moon than the average, non-astronomer does today. Its phases were tracked and used to measure the passage of time. People who lived close to the ocean carefully monitored the moon's phases in order to forecast tides. Farmers planted seeds and harvested crops based on the phases of the moon at certain times every year. Even social events were planned around the moon's phases, probably because when the moon is full you can see your companions almost as well as you could during the day.

Studying the moon is a hallmark of many elementary school science classes. Nevertheless, modern humans seem to truly understand very little about this sphere of rock that orbits our planet. First of all, most people tend to associate the moon with nighttime. **This is not helpful.** It is just as often above us during the day as it is during the night. It's just that during the day it is not nearly as noticeable.

A few basic facts:

- Its orbit around Earth is elliptical (oval), not a perfect circle.
- At the point of orbit when it is closest to Earth, **perigee**, the moon is 225,740 miles (363,300 kilometers or 0.0024 AU) away. At **apogee**, the farthest position, the distance is 251,970 miles (405,500 kilometers or 0.0027 AU).
- The diameter of the moon is 2,159 miles, or 3,475 kilometers, which is only about a quarter of the diameter of the Earth.
- Gravity on the moon is about 1/6th that on Earth.
- Surface temperatures there vary over a huge range: At the moon's equator, temperatures reach 260°F (127°C) during the day, when facing the Sun, and

then plunge to -280°F (-173°C) at night, when facing away from the Sun. In dark craters near the moon's poles, where the Sun never shines, the temperature is always around -400°F (-240°C).

It takes the moon 29 ½ days to rotate around its axis. It also takes the moon 29 ½ days to revolve around the Earth. This is not a coincidence, but a result **of tidal locking**. The moon and the Earth are rotationally synchronized so that the same side of the moon is always facing us. The result of this is that here on Earth we can only ever see one half of the moon. This is referred to as the **near side** of the moon. The **far side** of the moon can never be viewed from Earth. *The far side is not to be confused with the dark side.* The term **dark side** of the moon refers to the side of the moon that is facing away from the sun, which changes constantly, as all parts of the moon's surface are exposed to the sun's light at some point during the lunar cycle.

The moon appears to go through regular phases every month. On Earth a "day" is defined as the time it takes for us to be in the same spot relative to the Sun, which works out to be 24 hours. So the Earth is spinning around its own axis every 24 hours. The moon, meanwhile, is revolving around the Earth and completes a revolution around the Earth every 29 ½ days. Its orbit is in the same direction as the Earth's rotation, and so the Earth effectively "chases" the moon around its cycle. The result is that the lunar cycle is effectively 28 days, instead of 29 ½ days long. This is hard to imagine, but there are a

> The first photos of the far side came from the Soviet space camera Luna 3 in 1959. Then in 1968 the U.S. mission Apollo 8 brought three human beings to the far side. Their spaceship circled the moon ten times, allowing the astronauts to view the far side directly and take many photos. No humans have ever set foot on the far side of the moon.

few good websites with beautiful illustrations of this. Try **www.nasa.gov** and search on multi-media.

This same phenomenon explains why the moon appears to rise about 50 minutes later each day. For every day that passes here on Earth, the moon has moved just a little further along its orbit from where it was the day before. The moon will always rise in the east and set in the west, for the same reason why the Sun always rises in the eats and sets in the west.

PHASES OF THE MOON

The University of Texas' McDonald Observatory offers a neat, monthly illustration of the moon's phase every night in calendar format at www.stardate.org/nightsky/moon/.

Since the moon itself produces no light, what we see on Earth is the light of the Sun reflected off the surface of the moon. The new moon appears as no moon at all, because it is lined up between the Earth and the Sun. Each night the moon waxes (appears to get bigger) for 14 nights, until it reaches full moon, then wanes (appears to get smaller) for 14 nights, at which point it is a New Moon again. The waxing moon always shows its lighted portion on the right hand side of the moon, and the waning moon always shows its lighted portion on the left side of the moon.

Waxing crescent   ☽

Waning crescent   ☾

1) New Moon: This refers to the phase in the cycle when the moon becomes invisible. When the moon is lined up between the Sun and the Earth, we cannot see any of the Sun's light reflected, and so see no moon at all. This state occurs for one night, during which the moon is called "new". The night after a new moon, a thin, waxing crescent becomes visible. This visible part of the moon gets larger every night. A great video clip on how to better understand the moon's phases can be found at www.newtonsapple.tv/video.php?id=1671

Everyday Knowledge - Solar Eclipse

At certain, rare, new moon phases, the Sun, moon and Earth are lined up just right so that we see a **solar eclipse.** For a solar eclipse to occur, the moon must be lined up directly in the Sun's way. From Earth we see the sun with a blacked out circle (the moon) in the center of sunlight. Solar eclipses actually occur between two and five times a year, every year, but often they are only visible over the ocean or other uninhabited spot. More information on eclipses, including dates, can be found at www.eclipses.gsfc.nasa.gov/eclipse.html

2) First Quarter: The surface area of the moon reflecting sunlight to Earth continues to grow every night. On the eighth night after the new moon, we see a half circle moon. Unfortunately, this "half moon" is officially called the first quarter moon. Over the next few nights the moon is called a **waxing gibbous** moon, which describes the moon's appearance as it increases from a half to a full circle of light.

3) Full Moon: Whenever we observe a full moon, the moon is actually on the side of Earth opposite the sun, and so its entire face is reflecting the sun's light back to Earth. Because of these relative positions, a full moon rises about the time of sunset, and sets about the time of sunrise, for most places on Earth. After the full moon, we see the gibbous moon again (between full and half), and it gradually gets smaller (wanes) every night.

4) Third Quarter: Unlike in football, the third quarter here is also the last quarter. Here the waning moon goes from half to a crescent, then down to nothing, at which point the next new moon begins. It makes sense if you think about the fact that the two "half moon" phases are called First Quarter and Third Quarter because they occur when the moon is, respectively, one- and three-quarters of the way along its orbit from New Moon.

A **Lunar Eclipse** occurs when the Earth gets in between the Sun and the Moon. These can only happen during a full moon (think about it!). As the Earth passes between the Sun and the Moon it casts a shadow on the moon. Have you ever read a scary story that mentions the moon turning as red as blood? Sounds creepy. Actually this can - and does - occur although it has nothing to do with blood. As the Earth casts its shadow on the full moon, the moon begins to disappear from sight, then, it glows dark red during the mid-point of the eclipse. This is because the Sun's rays do not get totally blocked by the Earth. Remember — the Sun is much larger than the Earth. The rays get scattered around the Earth's surface. This refracting of sunlight through Earth's atmosphere causes the light to take on a reddish hue. This red light then gets reflected off the surface of the moon back to Earth, making the moon look red. It's easy to imagine how frightened our early ancestors must have been whenever this phenomenon occurred.

Everyday Activity – Moon Journal

Keep a moon journal with your kids. Every night *or day* for a month, look outside to check the location of the moon, what time it passes by a certain point, how big it is, what it's shaped like. Draw a picture of the moon in the journal. Remember the moon will become visible in the same spot on the horizon *about* 50 minutes later each day. Check out a moonrise table to be sure. For two weeks out of each month the moon will rise during daylight hours. It will be difficult to see, especially if the weather is cloudy.

The National Oceanographic and Atmospheric Administration publishes tables of moonrise and moonset. You can input your own location at the U.S. Navy's astronomical website and get exact times of moon rise and set, along with other astronomical data at www.aa.usno.navy.mil/data/docs/RS_OneYear.php. Make sure to account for daylight savings time differences.

OCEAN TIDES

Everyone knows that when a child asks why the ocean moves back and forth the correct answer is "it's because of the moon". But what, exactly does that mean? How can there be two high tides every day?

The moon is held in orbit around Earth because of our planet's much greater gravitational attraction, but the moon also exerts a gravitational pull on the Earth. The moon circles around the Earth, but the Earth also revolves around its own axis, and in doing so "follows" the moon around its orbit. Once the Earth rotates into its first view of the moon on the eastern horizon, which we call "moonrise", it takes about 12 hours and 25 minutes for the Earth to rotate through to the point where the moon "sets" on the western horizon. These two daily events generally represent the times of low tide for that location. The time when the moon is highest in the sky (known as the **zenith**), that is, directly overhead, generally represents **direct high tide** for that part of the world. This high tide results in the ocean's water filling up a larger space, and so water spills over land into the **tidal zone**. The water that is rising towards the moon has to come from somewhere. Since all of the world's oceans are connected, the oceans going through low tide are essentially giving up some of their volume to the rising tides.

In other words, the tides follow the moon. When the moon is high in the sky the tide also is high. When the moon is low on a horizon the tide is also low. But what is going on when you can't see the moon at all?

As the moon revolves around the Earth, one side of the Earth is facing the moon and one side is facing away. When part of Earth is experiencing its direct high tide, on the opposite side of the Earth, another high tide happens. The water on the opposite side experiences an **indirect high tide**, to compensate for the moon's gravitational tug. This second bulge is because of inertia, which counteracts the effect of gravity. In addition to the ocean, the Earth itself is getting pulled just a bit towards the moon. The water on the opposite side gets left behind to compensate, and the result is a high tide both on the portion of Earth facing the moon and the portion of Earth facing directly away from the moon. This indirect high tide is a lot harder to understand than the direct high tide. It helps to review the section on Newton's Laws of Motion. In a very simplified comparison, the indirect tide can be compared to sitting in a parked car. Imagine the Earth as the car, and the ocean water opposite the moon as the passengers in the car. When the Earth gets pulled towards the moon, the water on the opposite side of Earth experiences a pull in the other direction, just like the feeling of getting pushed back into the seat of the accelerating car.

With every passing day high tides occur *approximately* 50 minutes later than it did the day before. (Since the time difference between moonrise from one day

> **TWO NOTES OF CAUTION:**
>
> Since the moon's orbit is elliptical rather than a perfect circle, the occurrence of moonrise and moonset do not always happen exactly 50 minutes later every day, and so high and low tides also are not exactly 50 minutes later every day. To accurately figure out the exact moments of these events takes a lot of patience and a lot of calculations. That's why we use tables.
>
> And ... In real life the tidal situation is much more complicated. Because shorelines, islands, peninsulas and under water geologic formations get in the way of water, most areas of the Earth experience very complicated tidal patterns that don't fit this neat description. For an extreme example, the Gulf of Mexico only has one high and one low tide each day.

to the next is 24 hours and 50 minutes, then each day it will rise 50 minutes later than it did the day before.) If high tide is at 6:00 am and 6:25 pm one day, the next day high tide will be at 6:50 am and 7:15 pm. This pattern continues endlessly. It works out that approximately every two weeks high and low tides happen at about the same time of day.

The Northern Atlantic is famous for extreme differences in high and low tides, illustrated here in a fishing port in the Bay of Fundy, New Brunswick. Image courtesy of Samuel Wantman **www.commons.wikimedia.org/wiki/File:Bay_of_Fundy_High_Tide.jpg**

At some times, the high tides are much higher and low tides much lower than others. What causes this phenomenon? Many factors come into play. First, when the moon is at perigee, that is closer to Earth, its gravitational force is greater, and so high tides are higher and low tides lower. At apogee (farther from the Earth) both high and low tides are more moderate. The sun also affects tides through its gravitational pull on Earth. When the Earth is closer to both the moon (**perigee**) and the sun (**perihelion**), their gravitational effects are even more exaggerated. When the sun, Earth and moon are all lined up with each other in a line, as happens on nights of new moon and full moon, their effects are all working together, and so high tides are relatively higher. This is called **spring tide**. When the sun and the moon are at right angles with respect to Earth, the sun partially cancels out some of the moon's gravitational attraction, and so the tides are less pronounced. This is called a **neap tide**.

> The alignment of celestial bodies in a straight line, in this case the Sun, Earth, and Moon, is called **syzygy,** probably one of the coolest words in the English language!

There are an awful lot of strange, new vocabulary terms in this moon section. They have been included here mainly to help you help your kids learn the necessary terms for school. While useful, these strange sounding words often just turn kids off to the learning process. Don't get bogged down in a vocabulary fight. The most important thing is to understand the *concepts* of how the moon and the Earth interact. Try to instill an appreciation for the natural world and these never-ending cycles. This same rhythm of moonrise, the moon's sequence of phases, and the ebb and flow of the oceans all have been happening in exactly the same way, following the same rules of gravity and inertia, for billions of years. Learning what we call them now is not nearly as important as understanding them holistically.

Understand first, learn the words later.

Seasons

Why are there seasons? Why are some parts of the world cold when others are hot? Why is the weather near the Equator always the same? Most climate and weather issues will be discussed in the section on Meteorology, but the seasons are actually controlled by the position of our planet itself in relation to the sun, and so belong in this section. The cause of the seasons is commonly misunderstood to be that the Earth is closer to the sun, hence warmer, in summer and further away, hence colder, in winter. *This is not true*! The real reason why summer is hot and winter cold is the tilt of the Earth on its north-south axis. For half of the year, the North Pole is tilted slightly towards the Sun, and the South Pole is tilted away from the Sun. During the other half of the year the North Pole is tilted away and the South Pole is tilted towards the Sun.

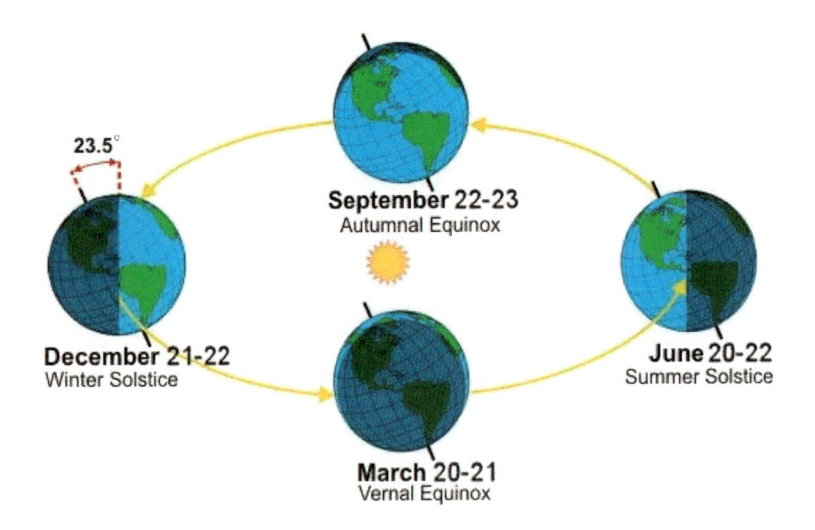

Image courtesy of National Oceanic & Atmospheric Agency
www.srh.noaa.gov/abq/?n=clifeatures_wintersolstice

As discussed above, all planets, including Earth, have elliptical or oval orbits, and at **perihelion** they are closer to the Sun than they are at **aphelion**. The Earth is, in fact, furthest from the sun in July and closest to the sun in January.

While the northern hemisphere is tilted towards the sun, the northern hemisphere is warmed. This causes it to be "summer" there. At the same time the southern hemisphere is tilted away from the sun, and there it is winter. Hence, summer and winter is opposite in the northern and southern hemispheres. In the northern hemisphere, the "summer solstice" occurs on or near to June 21st, which is the longest day of the year, because that day offers the most hours of sunlight of the year. At the North Pole the sun never sets set at this time. The sun appears to trace a circle around the horizon to mark the passing of a full 24 hour day. On or near June 21st the winter solstice occurs in the southern hemisphere. At the South Pole there is no sun visible at all for several days. Darkness is complete through the Antarctic snow.

Where in the World?

The Earth's climate regions are defined by their latitudes. **Latitude** is a measurement of distance around the globe in a north – south direction, away from the Equator, which itself is defined as 0° latitude. Each degree of latitude away from the Equator is equivalent to travelling about 69 miles (111 kilometers). Latitude is derived mathematically. An imaginary line drawn from the center of the Earth's core to the surface will form an angle with respect to the Equator. With the Equator itself defined as 0°, the North Pole is 90° North Latitude, and the South Pole is 90° South Latitude.

The Arctic Circle actually begins at latitude 66.6° North, and the Antarctic Circle begins at latitude 66.6° South. The 45th parallel (at 45° north latitude) is halfway between the Equator and the North Pole. This imaginary ring around the Earth runs through the North American cities of St. John, New Brunswick; Montreal, Quebec; and Portland, Oregon. It also runs through the Rhone Valley in France, through the middle of the Black and Caspian Seas, and through the city of Wakkanai, Japan.

Regions between 66.6° and 90° either north or south are described as being in the "Polar Regions", and are usually extremely cold. Regions between 23.5° and 66.5°, either north or south of the Equator, are described as "Temperate". Their temperatures, on average, are comfortable for people to live in but there is still a great deal of variation within these latitudes. No one could confuse the climate of Tucson, Arizona with that of Bangor, Maine,

North Pole = 90° North Latitude Latitude

45th Parallel North

Arctic Circle = 66.6° North

South Pole = 90° South Latitude South Latitude

45th Parallel South

Antarctic Circle = 66.6°

although both places are within this temperate zone. "Equatorial", also known as "Tropical", regions extend around the Equator, from 0° to 23.4° north or south. The tropical region is hot all the time, although specific regions experience variations in weather, such as wet or dry seasons, at the same times every year.

Longitude is not as important to the study of climate as latitude, but it should be introduced here while latitude is discussed. Longitude is a measurement of distance around the globe for anyone travelling in an east-west direction. These imaginary lines are drawn on maps from the North Pole to the South Pole. At the Equator longitude lines are 70 miles apart. At 80° North or South latitude, longitude lines are only 12 miles apart. (The area in between each longitude line is divided into minutes.) At the Poles the longitude lines meet.

So what does this have to do with the meteorology? Everything and nothing. The Earth has its own habits and doesn't really care what we call its different parts. However, having a common way to describe these parts helps people communicate in a commonly accepted way. The term 18° 29' N latitude, 66° 7' W

> Longitude begins in the city of Greenwich, England. The imaginary line that goes through this city is defined as 0° and is also called the **"Prime Meridian"**.
>
> Greenwich was chosen because it was the most important center of maritime business at the time that the first really accurate maps of the word were being drawn. Longitude was (and is) an extremely important reference point for sailors who travel large distances across oceans.

longitude will always describe the city of San Juan on the island of Puerto Rico, no matter who is describing it. Having a common understanding of climate zones makes communications about oceanic storms and other meteorological events easier too.

So, the Equator is hot, the Poles are cold, and every place in between is temperate. Summer happens when your part of the Earth is tilted towards the Sun, and winter happens when your part of the Earth is tilted away from the Sun. If these facts could explain everything about the weather, most meteorologists would be out of a job. The truth is that weather itself is incredibly complicated. Predicting what weather will be in the future is even more complicated. At any point there are many factors that contribute to a particular weather pattern, and these factors are constantly changing. The TV weather reporter might not always get his or her predictions right. But get your kids thinking about the different weather conditions they might experience every day. When things don't follow a neat pattern, try to instill in them an appreciation for the complexities involved.

Meteorology

What is climate? What is weather? What is the difference?

- **Climate** describes the long term conditions of a particular place, including the levels of moisture and dryness and the typical temperature range over time.
- **Weather** is the short term description of what is happening in a particular place at a specific time. What is the temperature? Is there any precipitation? What does the air pressure suggest about impending changes in the weather?

What makes rain fall? Why does it rain sometimes and snow other times? The obvious answer is that it snows when it's cold enough, but how cold is enough? Why do hurricanes happen in certain parts of the world and not others? What does it mean when the weatherman talks about "low pressure systems" or "fronts"? *Can I go swimming this afternoon?*

All these questions represent the wonders of everyday life. It is enlightening to learn how the answers to these questions were *originally* figured out. The technology we have at our fingertips today can answer that last question instantly, but we should instill in our kids an understanding for how this all works. An appreciation for the natural world, an understanding of how it all works the way it does, is one of the best gifts we can ever give to our children.

There are many factors that contribute to a particular set of weather conditions. As tempting as it is to connect one set of conditions with a particular weather forecast, this doesn't often work in real life. Any one factor will not accurately explain the actual weather that you experience. Many factors must be considered in order to make educated predictions of what the weather will be like over the next few days. In elementary school, kids should learn to understand that there are many forces out there. While they should be taught a basic understanding of what these forces are, it's way more important to give them an appreciation for the fact that it is complicated, sophisticated stuff. This is a problem kids (and adults) run into all the time. Too often science facts are taught (or reported) as a simple cause and effect: X happened so Y will follow. When Y doesn't happen, it is hard to reconcile the facts we were taught (or read about somewhere) with our real world situation. The actual science behind almost everything is way more complicated than X → Y, but it doesn't mean that these facts are faulty; it just means that the whole situation is very complex.

THE WATER CYCLE

All the water on the surface of the Earth has been here for about 4 billion (4,000,000,000) years. Since then the amount of water in oceans, lakes, rivers and atmospheric vapor has remained more or less constant. Water is constantly moving through the water cycle, but the total amount stays about the same.

About 71% of the Earth's surface is covered with water. There are about 326 million trillion (in scientific notation, 3.26×10^{20}) gallons of water on the surface of the Earth. Put in another term, that would be 332.5 million cubic miles. That being said, the location and condition of water changes and those details are extremely important to humans. Out of all this water, only about 1% is available as pure, fresh, liquid, drinkable water. Another 2% or so is frozen fresh water locked in glaciers. The other roughly 97%, such as salt water in the oceans, is not drinkable.

The study of water is rightfully a huge part of the curriculum in most elementary science classes. It's a fundamental part of the way the natural world works, and, luckily, it is relatively easy to demonstrate and understand.

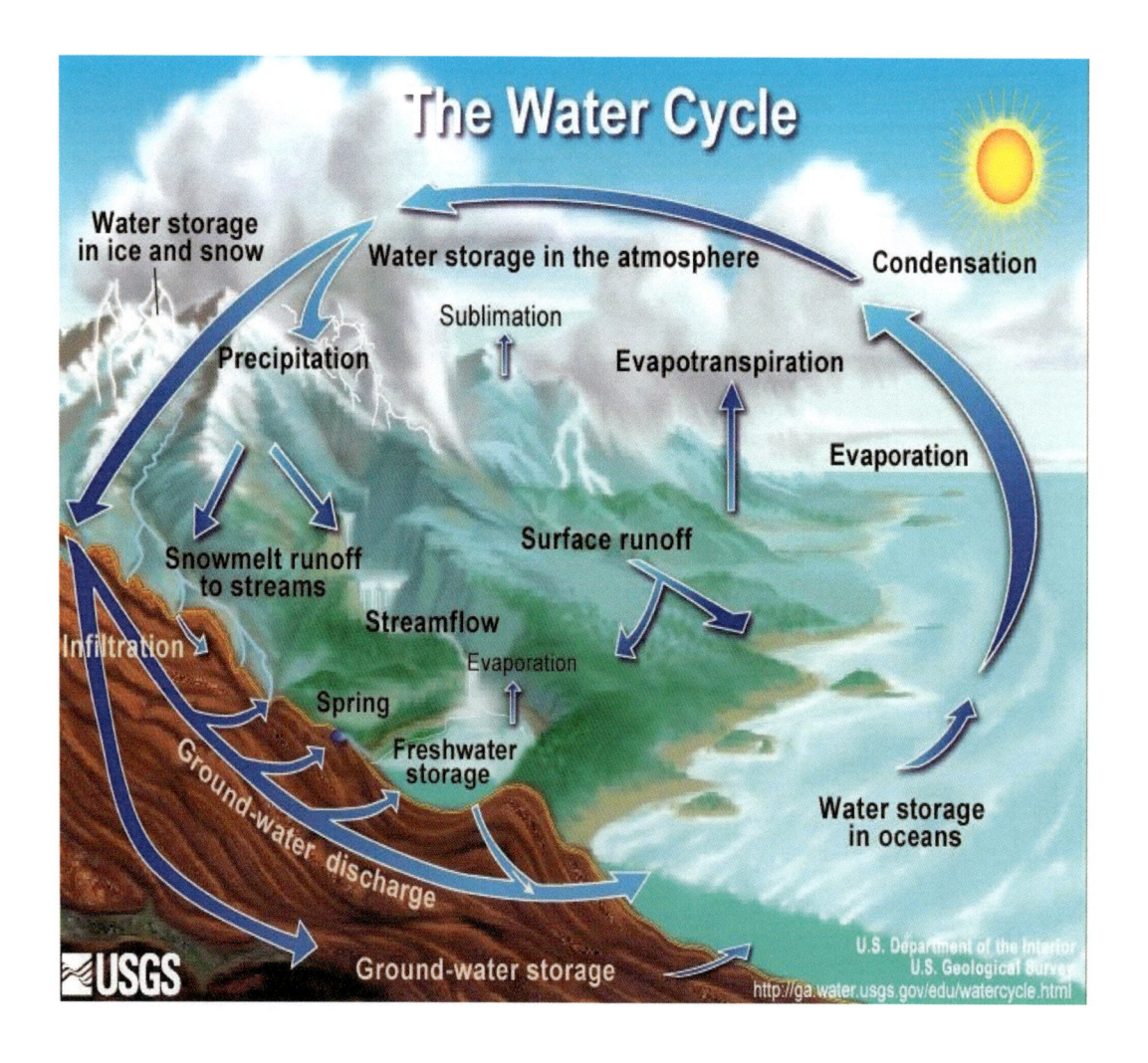

Everyday Experiment – Mini Water Cycle in a Dish

Here is a super easy demonstration that really drives home the water cycle concept. Get a glass casserole dish with matching glass cover. Any color glass will do, as long as it is transparent. Fill the dish half-way up with cold water. Cover and set in a sunny spot. The heat of the sun will cause some of the water to change from liquid to gas and **evaporate**. Depending on the strength of the sun (summer vs. winter) and the ambient (surrounding) temperature, you will be able to see droplets forming on the glass lid within a few hours. Since the dish is covered, the steam can't just evaporate into the surrounding air. When the steam hits the lid, it **condenses**, meaning it becomes liquid again. When enough of the **condensate** collects on the lid, the water droplets pool together, get heavy, and fall back down into the dish. In the real world this is known as **precipitation** or rain.

Here's an extra little twist. Find out two spots that are equally sunny but different in temperature. For example, if it's 40° F outside, and 70°F inside, get two identical dishes & lids, fill each half way with cold water. Make sure to put the same amount of water in each! (To insure the water is the same temperature, fill a pitcher with all the water you need, and leave it in the fridge overnight.) Fill the dishes with the same amount of water, cover them tightly, and place one on a table by a closed window where it gets full sunlight, and put one outside the same window. Check for condensation every 5 minutes or so and record when the first droplets appear on each lid.

Clouds

What is a cloud? A **cloud** is simply a huge mass of water vapor. If you have ever walked through **fog,** you have been inside a cloud. That's all it is. However, when you look at the sky you can see many different types of clouds over the course of a few days. If they are all just water vapor, what makes these clouds look different from each other? Their shapes and other characteristics depend on their temperature and altitude. Most clouds are white because the water droplets are reflecting all the light around them. When lots of clouds are tightly packed together, like before or during a storm, not much sunlight can get through so they appear darker grey instead of white. *(Go back to the section on Light and review that diagram of refraction & reflection of light in a water droplet.)*

Clouds are classified by their **altitude,** how high they are up in the sky:

- **Cirrus** - Cirrus type clouds are the highest. They are at least 18,000 feet (about 5,500 meters) above the Earth. Because they are so high, their water is held as ice crystals.

    Cirrus clouds are very high, thin, wispy things. In the olden days they were called "mares' tails" because they can resemble the tail of a horse blowing in the wind. These clouds themselves do not bring precipitation, but usually indicate that the weather will change in a day or so.

    Cirrostratus clouds are thin formations that spread across large portions of the sky. They form long, linear bands of clouds, earning the suffix " –stratus", which means "layered". These cloud formations appear during fair weather but often are a sign that rain or snow will start in 12 – 24 hours.

Cirrocumulus clouds are also thin formations that cover a large portion of the sky. From the ground they look a bit like fish scales. In fact, people used to refer to these clouds as "minnows' scales" or "mackerel sky". In the winter they usually indicate fair weather, but during hurricane season they can mean that a big storm is approaching.

- **Alto** - Clouds that form between 6,500 – 18,000 feet (roughly 2,000 – 5,500 meters) above the Earth are classified as Alto- clouds.

    Altostratus clouds are heavy looking, lower formations that cover most of the sky. They range from light to dark grey and have no discernible patterns. These indicate a period of continuous rain or snow will begin soon.

    Altocumulus clouds appear as puffy balls in a fairly regular pattern. Sometimes blue sky is visible between each puffball, but often the merge together. Sometimes the centers of these balls will be grey and the outside edges, where sunlight is penetrating through, appear bright white. When Altocumulus clouds are seen on summer mornings they generally indicate that thunderstorms will be coming through in the afternoon.

- **Stratus** – the lowest clouds, Stratus clouds are found lower than 6,500 feet (lower than 2,000 meters) above Earth.

Stratus clouds are dense, boring clouds that produce heavy mist or drizzle. These are very much like fog that is high above the ground. They are the lowest forming clouds.

Stratocumulus clouds look like a bunch of cumulus clouds crowded up together. They appear darker, since because of the crowding not much sun can get through, but they rarely bring rain themselves. Over time they can reform into **Nimbostratus** clouds, which are similar to Stratus clouds but they are even heavier and denser looking. They produce moderate amounts of rain or snow that falls for a long period of time.

- **Cumulus** – these clouds have vertical growth, meaning that they extend through at least two atmospheric layers.

    Cumulus clouds are the typical fair weather cloud. They are the ones that tend to look like funny animals or other forms and generally can be found scattered throughout an otherwise blue sky. Their bottoms are flat and their tops are rounded and puffy.

    Cumulonimbus clouds are the *Big, Bad* clouds! They are very tall, stretching as much as 40,000 feet high. Their tops can be shaved off by the action of strong winds and so appear flat or anvil shaped. These clouds can indicate that severe storms are approaching, in the form of thunderstorms, hail, heavy snow, or tornadoes.

Everyday Knowledge - Clouds

There are many wonderful websites that offer beautiful cloud images. But beware! If your student is doing homework on cloud classification, make sure that you use images and information from a reputable source. Don't just search the internet for "clouds"! Many amateur photographers upload their own photos and name the clouds based on inaccurate information. They may have the best of intentions, but no one is checking their facts. Here are some sources you can trust.

www.nasa.gov

www.pbs.org/wgbh/nova/labs/lab/cloud/

www.srh.noaa.gov/srh/jetstream/clouds/clouds_intro.htm

Cumulonimbus cloud - image courtesy of NOAA:
www.srh.noaa.gov/srh/jetstream/clouds/basicten.htm

Everyday Activity –

What Do Clouds Look Like?

It's always fun to look at clouds and imagine them to look like elephants and penguins and ice cream cones. It can be just as interesting to think about different types of clouds and how people used to use them to predict weather. As long as humans have been looking at the sky, we have tried to find signs that would help us to understand the world better, and make our lives easier. When everyone made their livings by hunting and gathering, farming, or fishing, knowing what to expect from the weather was extremely important. Even children, who spent most of their time outdoors, could recognize certain cloud formations. We know now that many different factors are in play when it comes to weather. But some patterns have been generally known throughout the centuries to be reasonably predictive.

Mares' Tails and Mackerel Scales Make Tall Ships Take in Their Sails - As mentioned above, the cirrus clouds (Mares' Tails) and cirrocumulus (Mackerel Scales) can indicate that over the next 24 hours or so there will be a front coming through and a storm will soon follow.   **Red Sky at Night, Sailors' Delight; Red Sky in Morning, Sailors Take Warning** - As the sun sets in the west, it will cast a reddish glow. If a high pressure area is moving in (and in the northern hemisphere weather generally moves from west towards east) then the high pressure will actually compress airborne particles of dust and smoke. With more particles for the sun's light to scatter off of, the sunset will appear even reddish, indicating that fair weather is approaching. When the sunrise glows red in the east, it generally means that a high pressure system is leaving (in other words, it is east of where you are) and a lower pressure system is arriving.   **When Clouds Look Like Rocks and Towers, the Earth Will Be Refreshed by Showers** - Those "bad boys", the cumulonimbus clouds, grow to gigantic heights. From the ground these clouds can easily be imagined to look like medieval towers made of white rocks. Refreshed might be a slightly euphemistic term for soaked!

BAROMETRIC PRESSURE

Weather reports often include references to "high pressure systems" or "low pressure systems", but what does this actually mean?

Air generally moves around the world in giant spinning **masses,** hundreds or thousands of miles wide. A **high pressure air mass** is surrounded by air of lower pressure, by definition. The air inside a balloon is at much higher pressure relative to the air outside the balloon. When a balloon pops, the air inside the balloon rushes out to get to a place of lower pressure. Likewise, on a much larger scale, as a high pressure air mass spins, the high pressure air spirals outward, to get to a place of lower pressure. The center of the high pressure mass then sucks air down from high altitudes to replace the lost air, and the process continues.

A **low pressure air mass** acts in the opposite way. Since the air around it, by definition, is at a higher pressure, that air wants to rush in towards the area of lower pressure. As the higher pressure air moves into the lower pressure air mass, the mass gets too full, and air gets pulled upward into higher altitudes. As this air rises, it cools, and any moisture in it condenses. This condensation creates clouds, which can bring rain or snow. That's why a low pressure system typically brings precipitation.

At any given time, the Earth is covered by these gigantic air masses floating around, each one doing its own thing. Each air mass has its own temperature, as well as its own pressure. An air mass that travels southward from the Arctic regions will be a lot colder than an air mass that is blowing northward from the mid-Atlantic. What happens when two air masses collide? They battle each other! The point of contact between a cold air mass and a warm air mass is called a **front.** This term was actually first used during World War I, when government scientists were trying to learn more about predicting the weather to help its fledging air force better navigate around storms. "Front" is the military term for the place where two armies do battle, and a weather front actually represents a gigantic, invisible battle that takes place over a particular territory in the air.

A **cold front** occurs when a cold air mass moves into the area occupied by a warmer air mass. Since cold air is denser than warm air, the colder air sinks, wedging itself under the warmer air and forcing the warm air up. As the warm air rises it cools, and whatever moisture had been in it condenses and falls out as rain or snow.

> Refer back to the Physics Chapter. The process of convection is described using the model of a pot of water heating on a stove. The same concepts apply here too.

A **warm front** occurs when a warm air mass moves into an area occupied by a colder air mass. In this scenario the warm air still rises above the cooler air, but it tends to happen more gradually. This gentle upward movement of the warmer air can also bring precipitation, but usually in a much milder form.

Everyday Example - Thunderstorms

You can easily imagine (and have probably experienced) this taking place. Think about a hot, muggy summer afternoon. The air is very **humid** (full of moisture) and still. You feel a cool breeze. The leaves on the trees blow upwards, revealing their paler shade of green underneath. Suddenly a great, cool wind sweeps past, followed within minutes by a blast of hard, driving rain. The next time you experience this situation, talk to your kids about the phenomenon of the cold air mass rushing underneath the warm air, forcing the warm air up where its moisture cools, condenses, and precipitates.

The **Jet Stream** is a "river" of air found high in the Earth's atmosphere, roughly 5 - 9 miles (8 - 15 kilometers) above the surface. The jet stream is initiated by temperature differences. Warmer air from the equatorial regions drifts towards the poles (toward the North Pole north of the Equator and southward on the southern side of the equator). If the Earth did not rotate then the jet stream would not exist, but, it does rotate and so, as it turns, these warm air masses are effectively rotated as well. The result is that in jet streams flow west to east in meandering, circular paths around the globe. The speed of these rivers of air varies between 80 - 140 miles / hour (129 - 225 km / hour). This is so powerful that airplanes cannot fly into it! Pilots do, however, take advantage of flying with the jet stream. That's why it always takes less time to fly eastward than it does to make the opposite flight. The jet streams are not fixed, but change their exact shape and local direction in response to many other factors. There are even reverse jet streams in the tropical regions, which bring warm air into Asia.

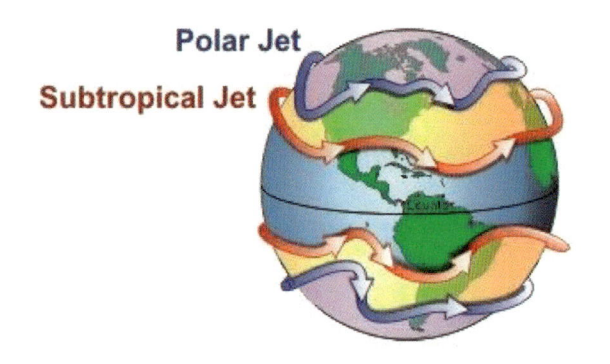

Stylized illustration of the major jet streams courtesy of the National Oceanic & Atmospheric Agency

www.srh.noaa.gov/jetstream/global/jet.htm

Wind

As describe above, the collision of air masses accounts for one of the reasons we experience wind here on the ground, but a lot more is going on.

Air will always move in a direction of high pressure to low pressure. When the sun comes up and warms an area of land, the air directly above that piece of land heats up (its temperature increases) therefore its pressure also increases. This air now has higher pressure. It wants to move to an area of lower pressure, and so it does. This movement of the air is called "wind". This phenomenon is called the **Pressure – Gradient Force**. The greater the difference between the air pressures, the stronger the force of the wind. Of course, whenever you deal with real world scenarios instead of neat little chunks of information, things get a bit more confusing. There are many other factors in play.

For hundreds of years it has been understood that wind is caused by the movement of air from hotter regions to colder regions, because *temperature and pressure are always proportional to each other*. That means that, all other conditions being equal, if one increases, the other will also increase. Refer back to this section in the Physics chapter for more information. When everything else stays the same:

- An increase in pressure will always cause an increase in temperature.
- An increase in temperature will always cause an increase in pressure.
- A decrease in pressure will always cause a decrease in temperature.
- A decrease in temperature will always cause a decrease in pressure.

> Evangelista Torricelli, an Italian scientist, is widely credited with the development of the barometer, in 1643. The Torr, which is a unit of pressure, as named after him. Actually several other scientists contributed to this understanding of air pressure, including his friend and mentor, Galileo.

Everyday Knowledge – The Wind Tunnel Effect

One real life factor that can effect what we feel on the ground is the "**wind tunnel** effect". Basically, if wind is blowing across an open field, there will be little or no difference in the speed of the wind at different spots on that field. However, if two huge buildings are erected on the field, with a narrow alley between them, the speed of the wind coming through that alley will be much greater than the wind blowing across the open field. (Cities in the Mid-West were built on the Plains, and so are often extremely windy places.) This is because the same *amount* of wind still blows across the field, but, in the second scenario, most of the wind's path is blocked by the buildings. The wind now must pass through the alley in between, and so the speed of the wind through the alley is much greater than the speed of the wind across the open field. It's kind of like a waterfall, which channels a lot of water in a river or pond through a very small outlet, thereby producing a very fast moving river of water. This phenomenon applies to natural obstructions like mountains as well as to man-made buildings, and can be experienced in environments as different as city streets and mountain passes.

The Windy City

"Chicago Grant Park night pano" by Daniel Schwen - Own work
www.commons.wikimedia.org/wiki/File:Chicago_Grant_Park_night_pano.jpg#mediaviewer/File:Chicago_Grant_Park_night_pano.jpg

Everyday Knowledge -
The Wind Chill Effect

People love to talk about the wind chill. In colder climates, the winter temperatures can be impressively low, but even more so when the wind chill factor is taken into account. This is a measure of the temperature compounded by how cold your *unprotected* skin would feel because of the wind. Meteorologists use a standard mathematical formula to come up with this value. However, it is not the actual temperature. Remember the description of how a convection oven works? Well, your body produces a very thin "envelope" of heat (just the way a casserole baking in the oven retains an "envelope" of its own temperature.) When outdoors on a windy day, the wind will blow away this envelope, and so any uncovered skin gets cold a lot faster than it would on a calm day with no wind. But it is not the real temperature. If you put two thermometers outside on a cold and windy day, one exposed to the wind and the other protected by a wall, they will both still read the same temperature. You probably have done this experiment already - think about your car's dashboard readout of temperature. The car's speed has no effect.

The wind chill factor is important if you plan on being outdoors for a long time, with any skin exposed. Under those conditions, wind chill will accelerate frostbite, and should be taken seriously.

More Interesting Wind Facts:

Trade Winds — So named because they enabled the trading routes of sailing ships hundreds of years ago. When countries had to actually send ships to another country to get exotic food, spices, metals and cloth, getting from point A to point B was a very big deal! Faster trade routes were aggressively sought, and once discovered, used to make these sailing trips as efficient and safe as possible. In the Northern

Hemisphere, these winds blow from northeast to southwest towards the Equator, and in the Southern Hemisphere they blow from southeast to northwest, also towards the Equator. These winds converge in the **Inter-tropical Convergence Zone.** This clashing of major wind patterns causes many thunderstorms in equatorial regions.

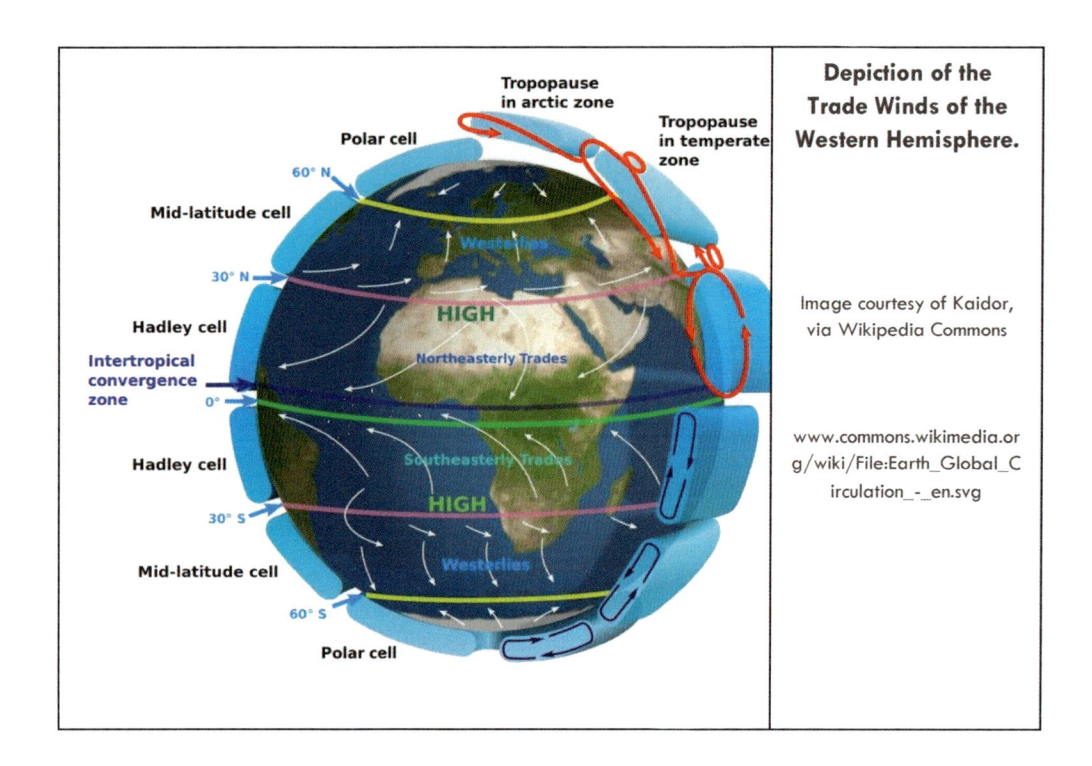

Depiction of the Trade Winds of the Western Hemisphere.

Image courtesy of Kaidor, via Wikipedia Commons

www.commons.wikimedia.org/wiki/File:Earth_Global_Circulation_-_en.svg

Doldrums - These are regions near the Equator where wind generally doesn't blow at all. They are areas of calm or very light winds. They were a disaster for the sailors in those trading ships. If a ship got stuck in these regions, the crew was in danger of running out of food and supplies before they could get to a port. This is where the saying "stuck in the doldrums" comes from, which describes someone who is too bored or lazy or sad to get anything done.

Prevailing Westerlies – Did you ever notice that the wind usually blows from west to east? Across the landmass of the United States, the Prevailing Westerlies are the predominant wind system. They are the reason that weather generally moves from west to east across the U.S. A large low pressure system that brings lots of rain or snow to the Midwest will usually bring lots of rain or snow to New England over the next few days. (Not always, because there are other factors that also contribute to the weather, but most of the time.) In fact, wind blowing from east to west often signifies an aberration from this prevailing system in the form of a storm coming through.

Cyclones

The planet's most destructive storms, cyclones are huge thunderstorms that spin. They are called **cyclones** in the Southern Hemisphere, **typhoons** in Asia, and **hurricanes** in the Atlantic region, but they are essentially the same type of storm. All are characterized by swirling clouds and very high winds. Cyclones form over oceans in the hot regions close to the Equator (although they rarely exist within $5°$ latitude of the Equator). During the warmest months of the year, huge amounts of seawater evaporate. As this water vapor rises to where the air temperature is cooler, the vapor condenses into huge cloud formations. Soon the moisture is released, and falls back to Earth as precipitation.

Imagine being able to look down on the Earth from above the North Pole. You would see that our Earth rotates on its axis in a counterclockwise direction. (It rotates clockwise if you imagine watching the Earth from above the South Pole.) This rotation causes wind to "bend". Think of riding on a merry-go-round with a friend sitting directly opposite you. If you toss a ball directly toward your friend, the ball will travel in a straight line. However, since your friend is moving on the merry-go-round, it will appear that the ball curves away. Wind also curves because of the Earth's rotation. Of course, in the merry-go-round example the ball simply goes straight — it doesn't bend; it's the kids who are moving. But standing on the surface of the Earth, we do not perceive our movement. What we perceive instead is the movement of the wind around us. This is called **The Coriolis Effect,** and it is most obvious when studying cyclones. North of the Equator, these storms spin in a counterclockwise direction. In the Southern Hemisphere, they spin in a clockwise direction.

Hurricane Sandy Over Cuba

www.nnvl.noaa.gov/GOESEast.php. Licensed under Public domain via Wikimedia Commons - www.commons.wikimedia.org/wiki/File:Sandy_Oct_25_2012_0400Z.JPG#mediaviewer/File:Sandy_Oct_25_2012_0400Z.JPG

> This natural phenomenon was named after Gustave – Gaspard Coriolis, who first described it in 1835.
>
> Incidentally, the Coriolis Effect is not demonstrable using a sink drain. That is a bit of misinformation that has taken on a life of its own. The direction that a sink drains (clockwise or counter-clockwise) is a function of the design of the sink and drain, not any global effect.

Many of these storms begin and end over the open ocean, where they do no damage. However, when the forces of the Earth blow a cyclone towards land, lots of bad things can occur. Coastal regions are particularly vulnerable to their damage. Why do these storms never affect areas that are far inland? Because the storm needs a constant re-supply of evaporating water to feed the clouds. Once over land, a hurricane will lose its intensity because it has no more water to pull up.

Cyclone Classification - the Saffir - Simpson Scale		
Category	Wind Speed (miles / hour)	Expected Damage
1	Wind speed of 75 – 95	Can break tree branches and damage coastal structures like piers and docks
2	Wind speed of 96 - 110	Can pull shingles of roofs and break windows. Unprotected boats are in danger. Trees can be damaged.
3	Wind speed of 111 - 130	Small buildings in danger. Mobile homes can be destroyed.
4	Wind speed of 131 - 155	Significant damage to large and small buildings. Coastal flooding and erosion of beaches.
5	Wind speed greater than 155	Massive damage to buildings of all sizes. Flooding of all lower floors of buildings near coast.

TORNADOES

In contrast to cyclones, which are associated with the oceans and coastal regions, tornadoes generally are an inland phenomenon. These are spinning funnels of air that drop down from thunderstorms. Like hurricanes they are also rated on a 5 point scale based on their wind speed. This is called the **F scale**, in honor of Theodore **Fujita**, who devised the system in 1972. This was updated in 2007 to account for the more violent storm systems of recent years. Below are the updated, or "Enhanced" Fujita values.

	Enhanced Fujita Scale
F1	Wind speed of less than 86 - 110 miles / hour
F2	Wind speed of 111 - 135 miles / hour
F3	Wind speed of 136 - 165 miles / hour
F4	Wind speed of 166 - 200 miles / hour
F5	Wind speed of over 200 miles / hour

At any point in time there are many factors that contribute to a particular weather pattern. Wind and water vapor play huge roles in creating the weather of any given place on any particular day. These factors are constantly changing.

Weather forecasting is a difficult and complicated science, and the TV weatherman might not always get the predictions right. But try to get your kids thinking about different aspects of the weather conditions they experience. When things don't seem to follow neat pattern of cause and effect, try to think about the reasons why what you observe is different from what you expected. Above all, try to instill an appreciation for the Earth as a complex system of forces all working together to create the world as we know it.

Geology

Geology is the study of what our planet is made of. Knowledge of geology provides important and relevant information on how to support our societies. Why is one part of a country fertile and another barren? Certain crops grow extremely well in some areas, and not very well in others, even when climates are similar. Where are oil and gas and mineral deposits hidden underground? Where can we build strong, stable buildings? Where is there a large enough ground water aquifer to sustain a growing population?

Geology also reveals the history of our planet. Rocks can tell us what the Earth looked like millions of years ago, what was going on then, and what has changed in the meantime. Volcanic eruptions, avalanches, glaciers, ocean waves, river currents and even wind have moved rocks around the Earth for billions of years. Rocks can also be changed from one type into another through chemical reactions, like iron turning into rust. They can be melded together and ripped apart by natural forces. Of course, as the molecular configurations of each substance morphs from one type of rock into another, always remember that the **elements** that the rocks are made of do not change, nor does their mass increase or decrease.

(In the Chemistry section we discussed the difference between and atom and a molecule and how, as chemical bonds are made and broken to create different molecules, the actual atoms of each element involved must stay the same.)

So, when did it all start?

Geology actually starts with *astronomy*. A few billion years ago, within the Milky Way galaxy, a gigantic cloud of gas and dust began to collapse into itself. As this gas cloud got smaller, its density increased, and, therefore, its temperature increased too. At the center of this cloud, the hottest spot, our Sun began to form. As this early Sun continued to get denser and heavier, its gravitational power increased. It began to pull everything else in the cloud towards itself. The rest of the cloud — atoms and molecules and charged particles — started to spin around this proto-Sun.

Image of our Solar System as a Proplyd - courtesy of the Keck Observatory — artist's rendition

The **Solar System** was starting to take shape. (Review the paragraph on proplyd formation in the astronomy section.)

During all this spinning and colliding, particles that were similar to each other began to coalesce (stick together) and lighter particles began to circle around heavier ones. This was the birth of the planets. As our Earth started to take shape, the densest atoms, chiefly iron (Fe), and some other metallic atoms, formed the core of the planet. Over the next few million years, other, less dense, elements whirling around the core formed the Earth's mantle and crust. These elements — oxygen (O), silicon (Si), aluminum (Al), etc. - combined in many different ways to form all the minerals and rocks that we still have today. Lighter elements formed the outermost layers of Earth, including the early atmosphere. By about 4.5 billion years ago, the planet was formed, although it would not be recognizable (or habitable) by today's standards. Land started to form into continent- sized areas about 2.5 billion years ago. Over eons of time the land mass broke into pieces and moved around. Scientists believe that there were several epochs of land masses coming together and breaking apart. The most recent phase is termed **"Pangaea",** for "Whole Earth", Pangaea describes an era when most solid land was all clustered together on one part of the planet about 225 million years ago. This Pangean super-continent began to break apart into the continents we know today through a process called **Plate Tectonics** (described below). In fact, the Earth's land is constantly moving around. What we recognize today as continents and islands are just a snapshot of the current positions of the land. Millions of years in the future, our world's continents, coastlines, mountains and valleys will look quite different.

PERMIAN
225 million years ago

TRIASSIC
200 million years ago

JURASSIC
150 million years ago

CRETACEOUS
65 million years ago

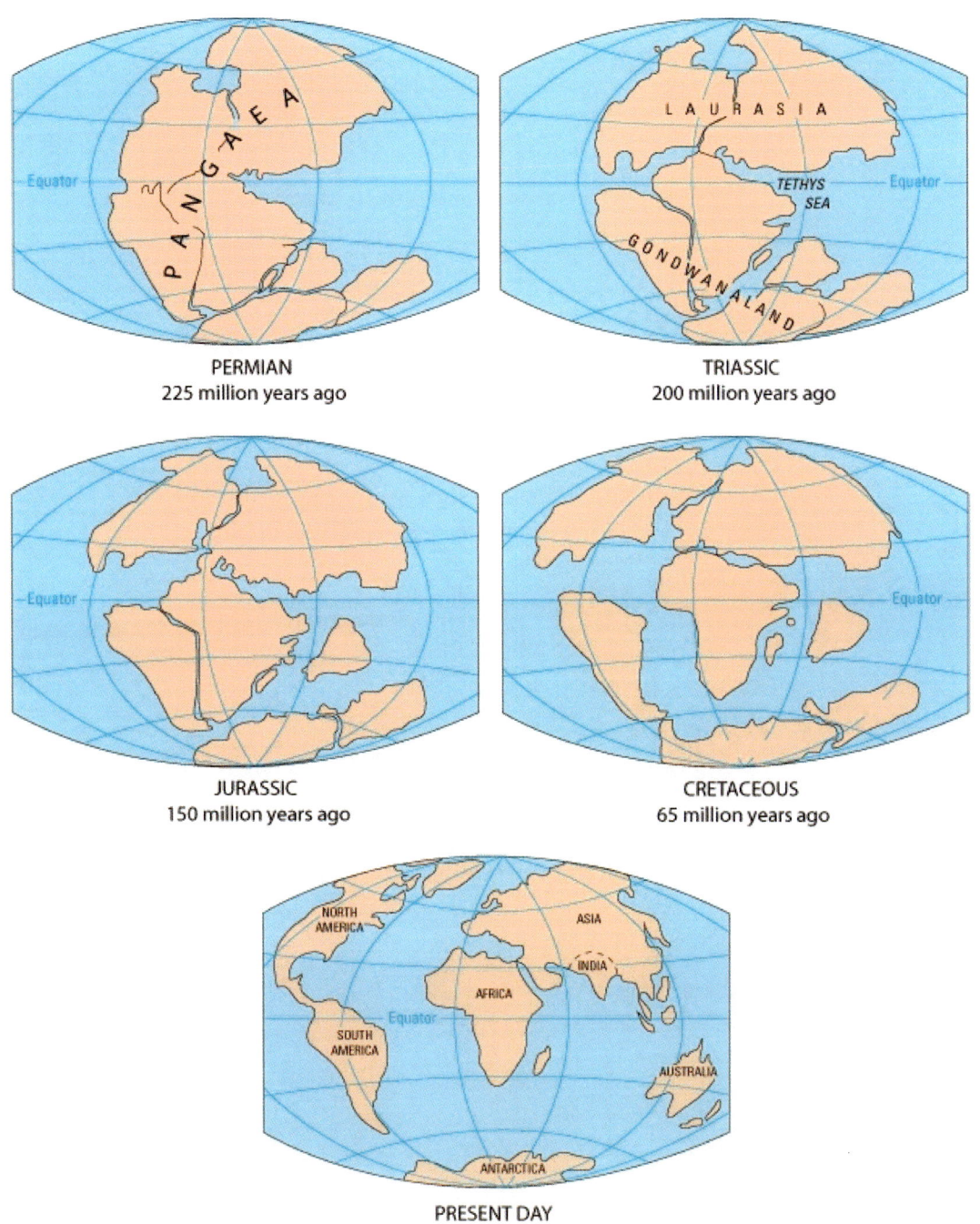

PRESENT DAY

Image courtesy of the U.S. Geologic Survey
www.pubs.usgs.gov/gip/dynamic/historical.html

PLATE TECTONICS

This field of science came into existence during the 20th century through the work of several extremely open minded men. In 1912 **Alfred Wegener** did something that many children have, at some point in their school day, considered doing themselves: he took a map of the world, cut out all the continents, and tried to fit them together, like a jigsaw puzzle. It worked! The "puzzle pieces" fit together quite nicely. Not only did these large puzzle pieces fit, but this concept of **Pangaea** (Whole Earth) explained how various rock and mineral deposits found in Brazil were very similar to those found in western Africa. It even explained how animals and fossils found in Africa looked a lot like those found in South America. The puzzle shapes matched up, and the pictures on the puzzle matched up as well. Wegener proposed the theory of **Continental Drift** to explain how a single, huge land mass separated over time to form the seven continents that we know today. But Wegener was ahead of his time. It took another four decades for technology to be able to prove his ideas were correct

The Mid-Atlantic Ridge

Image courtesy of **www.pubs.usgs.gov**

During World War II, a geologist named Harry **Hess** was working as a commander for the U.S. Navy. His ship was equipped with a new depth measuring device so that he could map the under-ocean terrain to better prepare troops who would be landing on enemy beaches. To his astonishment he was able to see mountains and valleys under the water. Especially notable was a **"Mid-Atlantic Ridge"** of mountains that ran north – south under the Atlantic Ocean for thousands of miles, and basically following the coastal contours of the land masses of Europe, North America, South America and Africa.

Thanks to the contributions of many scientists over time, we now know that hot **magma** from under the Earth bubbles up through the center of this underwater ridge. When it reaches the top of the ridge, the lava runs down the sides in both directions, cools and hardens. **In fact, scientists have been able to show that the rock formations on the eastern and western shores of the Atlantic are older than those closer to the Ridge,** *and* **those equidistant to the center of the ridge are of an equal age.** The rock near the center of the ridge is the youngest, meaning it has most recently bubbled up from under the Earth's crust.

Pahoehoe Lava on the Hawaiian Islands during eruption and after it has cooled.

Both images courtesy of J.D. Griggs via
www.en.wikipedia.org/wiki/Lava

The force of this rising magma was the reason that the land masses broke apart from each other about 200 million years ago. This research finally provided conclusive evidence for Wegener's theory of continental drift. This oozing of magma from the Mid-Atlantic Ridge, and the continued separation of the continents, happens almost continuously and is still happening today, at a rate of about 1 inch / year, or about 15 miles every million years.

> Magma and Lava are basically the same stuff - molten rock. It is called "magma" while still underground, and becomes "lava" when it erupts onto the Earth's surface.

All together there are fifteen tectonic plates covering the Earth, and they loosely correlate to what we recognize as the continents, the oceans, and the major island groups. There are three types of boundaries between these plates: **Divergent**, **Transform**, and **Convergent**.

- Divergent boundaries occur at the point where plates are moving away (diverging) from one another. Examples are the Mid-Atlantic Ridge and the Great Rift Valley in Africa.

- Transform boundaries occur where two plates slide along each other, creating a great deal of friction in the process. An example of this type is the San Andreas Fault in California, the site of much earthquake activity.

Aerial view of the San Andres Fault

Image courtesy of
www.commons.wikimedia.org/wiki/File:Kluft-photo-Carrizo-Plain-Nov-2007-Img_0327.jpg

- Convergent boundaries can be either **subductive**, meaning one plate pushes under another, or **collision**, meaning that two plates jam against each other. An example of subductive action is the Andes Mountains in western South America. Over millions of years, a Pacific oceanic plate was subducted underneath the South American continental plate, resulting in the massive and magnificent Andes Mountains. Look at a map – it's easy to imagine this action taking place!

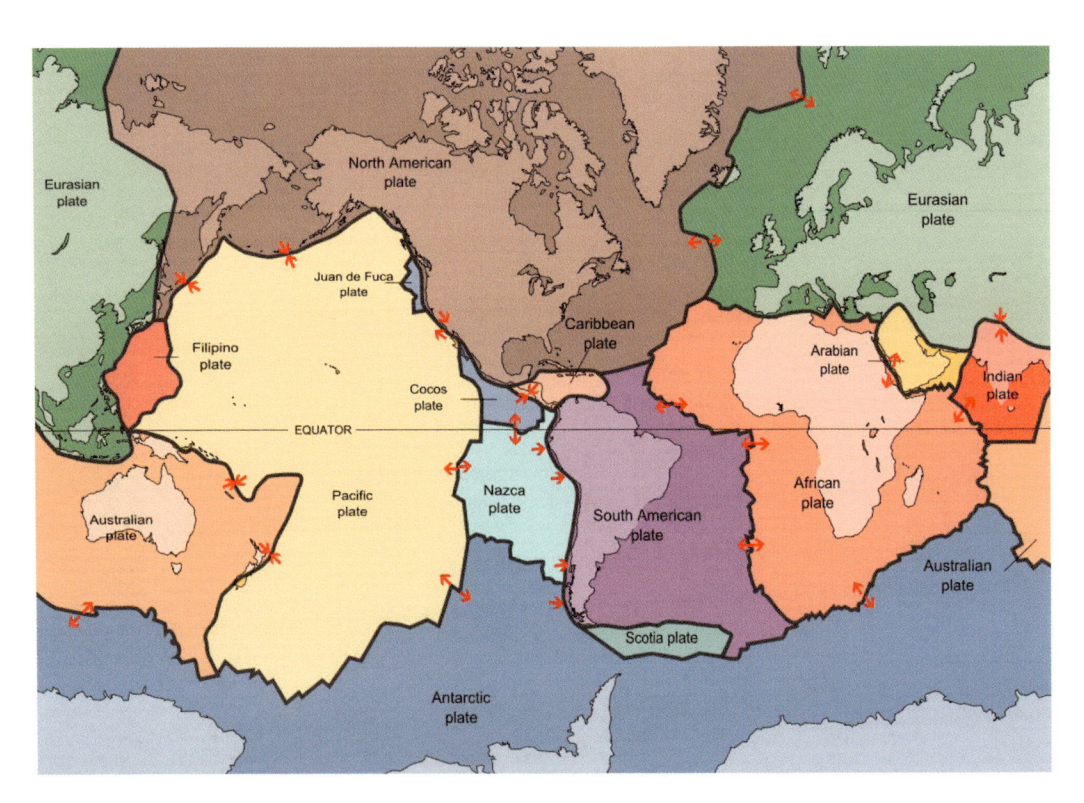

Tectonic Plates of Planet Earth

Image courtesy of the U.S. Geological Survey, via www.pubs.usgs.gov/gip/dynamic/slabs.html

An example of **collision boundary** can be found in the Himalaya Mountains in Asia. These continental plates are still pushing against each other. Mt. Everest, the world's highest mountain, continues to get taller, albeit by only a few millimeters a year.

On a very large scale, plate tectonics explains volcanoes, earthquakes and mountain building. On a smaller scale these forces explain the rock cycle and how forces within the Earth result in all the beautiful pebbles you might find on the beach, the granite curbstones that line city streets or the marble used to create some of the world's most beautiful sculptures.

Rocks & Minerals

What's the difference? **Rock** is a generic term. Any hard, solid, naturally occurring chunk can be thought of as a rock, but actually rocks come in three distinct types: **sedimentary, metamorphic,** and **igneous** which will be described in detail in the next section. The word **mineral** refers to the actual chemical compounds that a rock is made of. There are hundreds of defined mineral compositions. For example, quartz is made up of silicon and oxygen molecules bonded to each other in a particular pattern. Different environmental conditions can change the pattern of molecules, as when iron turns into iron oxide, also known as rust. This happens when the oxygen atoms from water molecules react with the iron atoms.

> *Everyday Activity*
> *Sand Art*
>
> Help your kids understand sedimentation and create some lovely artwork to display in your home.
>
> Sand Art kits are inexpensive and available at most toy or craft stores. Explain how the laying down of layers of sand is exactly what happens under the ocean. Get creative and add a few layers of crushed seashells or pieces of pine needles, seeds, or other organic matter.
>
> Show them pictures of the Grand Canyon and point out the similarities between the (now) exposed walls and their little creations. The process is essentially the same, even if the scale is extremely different.

Sedimentary: For over about three billion years, mud and sand have been washing down hills into streams, lakes or seas. Whatever the final destination, as these grains of minerals enter the water, they sink to the bottom and, over time, are covered with additional layers of mud and sand. Typically the bodies of aquatic organisms — micro-

> ## Everyday Activity
> ## Rocks Online
>
> If your kids develop a special interest in rocks and minerals, or you are looking for research project or science fair ideas, try searching Google Images for rocks or minerals or specific topics like intrusive igneous rock. Wikipedia is a great place to start. Additionally, try searching at sites designated .edu or .gov so that the pictures you get will come with reliable information. By limiting your searches to educational or government institutions you can be assured of accurate classification and background information, in addition to pretty pictures. Try looking for the following: basalt columns, basalt pillows, garnet gneiss, obsidian, pyrophyllite, or labradorite to view some beautiful creations of Nature.

organisms and plankton as well as shellfish, coral and larger fish, also sink to the bottom. As layer upon layer builds up and get compressed by the weight of the water above, the sediment becomes sedimentary rock. Examples of sedimentary rock include sandstone (rock made of sand) and limestone (rock made of lime, a.k.a. calcium carbonate, the kind of lime you put on your lawn.)

Metamorphic: Metamorphic rocks are rocks that have been changed from one type into another because of great forces of the Earth. The pressure caused by great volumes of water or by geologic plates moving together or by volcanic eruptions is so great that rocks are literally melted or forced to combine with other rocks, resulting in a new type. "Meta" means changed and "morpho" means form, hence the name. Just like when a caterpillar undergoes metamorphosis to become a butterfly, rocks can also undergo metamorphosis to change into something qualitatively different. As in the biological example, the actual composition stays the same, but the way the elements are combined with each other changes dramatically, resulting in something that looks very different from what it started as. Examples of metamorphic rocks are slate (used in old-fashioned roofs and blackboards and paving stones) marble, gneiss and schist. Marble is metamorphosed limestone. **Gneisses** and **schists** typically can be recognized by wavy bands of different types of rock that has been squeezed together under very high temperature and pressure. They also often have chunks of colorful crystals inside because many minerals will only form crystals under conditions of extremely high temperature and pressure.

Samples of Gneiss and Schist - Gneiss' wavy lines and schist's garnet crystal both formed as a result of intense pressure eons ago. Photos courtesy of Georgia State University via www.hyperphysics.phy-astr.gsu.edu/hbase/geophys/gneiss.html and Wikipedia: www.commons.wikimedia.org/wiki/File:Almandine.jpeg

Igneous: Igneous means "made by fire". (Think of the word "ignite"). There are two distinct kinds of igneous rock, extrusive and intrusive. In either case, these rocks are formed from **magma** deep within the Earth that has come up to the surface and hardened. Magma is liquefied rock, but the actual chemical composition can vary. When conditions are right for this stuff to rise up out of the ground, magma becomes **lava.**

Extrusive igneous rock is magma that came out of a volcano, and then cooled into rock on the surface of the Earth. **Basalt**, cooled and hardened lava, is an example of extrusive, igneous rock. **Pumice** is lava that cooled so fast that air bubbles were trapped inside of it. **Pyroclastic** rocks are chunks of lava that were forcibly thrown out of a volcano, hardening as they flew through the air. (Most nine year olds think this is pretty cool!) Simply getting your child to realize that this chunk of rock they are holding in their hands actually came rocketing out of the earth in a fiery explosion, can go a long way towards engaging their interest!

Intrusive igneous rock has less exciting history, but ends up looking much more beautiful. In this case the magma bubbles up from a volcanic vent, but doesn't quite make it out of the vent and solidifies while still underground. Because it doesn't actually reach the surface, it cools very, very slowly. This slow cooling process gives the molten minerals a long time to form crystals, and for these crystals to arrange themselves in nice patterns. **Granite** is a common example of intrusive igneous rock. Its familiar grainy texture is a direct result of the slow cooling process. Only after mining, or many years of erosion, is this type of rock visible.

Weathering is the process of rocks being chemically and / or physically changed by the forces of wind, water or other rocks. On the Earth's surface, rocks are constantly being bombarded with rain, wind, the flow of streams or waves, etc.

- **Chemical weathering** is the process of water actually changing the molecular configuration of the rock. For example, iron becomes iron oxide when exposed to moisture. In that case, four atoms of iron (Fe) react with two molecules of oxygen (O_2) to form two molecules of iron oxide, or rust (Fe_2O_3).
- **Mechanical weathering** is the process of wind and water breaking off bits of a rock, grinding it down over time. Beautiful examples of this can be seen in

river stones that have been tumbled by waves or rapids into fine, rounded specimens.

- **Erosion** is the process by which wind and water actually break down rocks. Over time, erosion can make mountains smaller and move entire hillsides into the valleys below. Wind and water can transport rocks, sand and soil downhill into bodies of water, where, over time, they become sediment and could even fill in the bottom of a lake or pond, turning it into dry land.

Even when rocks are broken up into tiny grains of sand, the *elements* that make up the rock are still there, and they will continue to exist no matter what phase of the cycle they are in.

The Rock Cycle

Basically, igneous rock is brought up from underground by a violent geologic event, such as the eruption of a volcano. The resulting lava hardens and, over time, bits and pieces of this volcanic rock wear away and get washed or blown downhill. These bits eventually get mixed with other bits of rock and become dirt or soil. Eventually this all ends up in a body of water. Because of gravity, the bits of rock now get deposited in the bottom of a lake or stream bed, or at the bottom of the ocean. If conditions are right, namely if there is enough water to create huge amounts of pressure on the sediment, it gets compacted into sedimentary rock. Layers of sedimentary rock build on top of each other over millions of years. Sometimes the bottom layers are under so much pressure that they metamorphose (change) into metamorphic rock. This is often

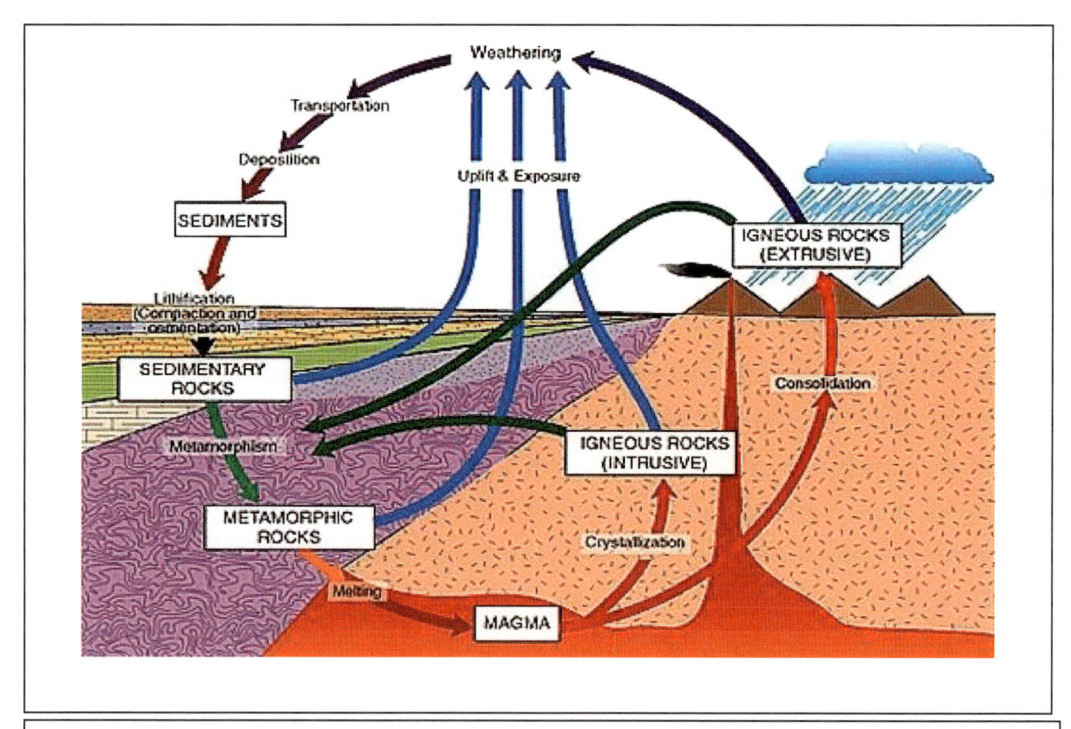

Image courtesy of Dr. Nicholas Short's Remote Sensing Tutorial, NASA Outreach Service
www.rst.gsfc.nasa.gov/Sect2/Sect2_1a.html

refer to the "rock cycle", but it should be understood that this is not necessarily a circular process. As with most of the natural world, what really happens is far more complicated. Some chunk of rock may actually complete a full circle, obediently going through each phase in order, but most do not. As illustrated in the diagram, sometimes igneous rocks can go straight into a metamorphic phase. Under certain conditions, the water above the sedimentary rock evaporates or drains, revealing the rocky layers underneath. But the concept of a cycle is important to drive home the message that the **elements** that make up rocks are here to stay. And... remember those are the same elements that were created in a star's core or during a supernova explosion, found their way into our solar system, and became the foundation of Earth...

Everyday Activity - Rocks in Real Life

Always be on the lookout for special places. Some places, if you have the privilege of traveling there, offer amazing geologic formations to explore. In the United States, the Grand Canyon is the most famous. Zion and Bryce Canyon National Parks offer spectacular examples of geologic formations. On the East Coast, the Canadian Maritime Provinces are well known for huge tides that reveal underwater rock structures when the water ebbs. Evidence of glaciers can be found in most of the northeast quadrant of the United States. Even driving on most major highways (depending on your location) can offer a glimpse into the geologic past of that region. Look for areas where engineers blasted through bedrock to lay the road, and you can see cliffs of what bedrock remains. The U.S. Geologic Survey (**www.USGS.gov**) and the National Park Service (**www.NPS.gov**) are wonderful sources for maps and information that can be searched by region.

Garden of the Gods in Colorado Springs, CO
Photo courtesy of Greverod via www.commons.wikimedia.org/wiki/File:Garden_of_the_Gods_03.jpg

"Jaws" Rock formation in Nevada

Photo courtesy of John Fowler via www.commons.wikimedia.org/wiki/File:Jaws_(5730281045).jpg

Giant's Causeway in Northern Ireland.

Photo courtesy of www.en.wikipedia.org/wiki/File:Causeway-code_poet-4.jpg

Fossil Fuels

One very special kind of sedimentary rock is coal. Coal is essentially the element carbon, with varying amounts of other stuff, and it is formed from material that was once alive – plants and animals and microorganisms that have been buried and compacted over millions of years. The basic stages of coal formation are as follows:

When biological material accumulates in swamp-like environments, it gets compressed into **peat,** which is an extremely dense sort of vegetal matting. People in some parts of the world use peat as a source of fuel for small home fires. It can be cut into chunks and carried fairly easily, but it doesn't have a lot of stored energy, and it generates a lot of smoke.

If peat is buried for many, many more years, and compressed further, the next stage it goes through is **lignite**, which is the softest form of coal. This is a better fuel, but, like peat, still makes a very smoky, smelly fire because of all the contaminants present.

With much more time and compression on the sediment, this material next becomes **bituminous coal.** This is considered "real" coal, and is useful as a fuel on a large scale. It burns with less smelly smoke than peat or lignite, but still produces lots of nasty byproducts as it burns.

Finally, in areas where the Earth has gone through the tectonic process of mountain building, this extreme pressure can produce a type of coal called **anthracite.** Anthracite is the purest form of coal, meaning it is mostly carbon, with very few impurities. It is the best for burning as fuel because it generates the most heat per pound and also produces the least amount of noxious byproducts relative to other coal types.

Today coal is one of the major sources of fuel used to run electricity generators. So, if you think about the process, every time you plug in your computer, you are using the remains of prehistoric organisms to power your 21st century lifestyle!

The same basic concept goes for our other hydrocarbon energy sources: gasoline, heating oil, natural gas. All these chemicals are hydrocarbons, meaning they are compose of hydrogen, carbon, and, also, oxygen. All these resources are the products of the decayed bodies of ancient, once-living cells.

Contrary to popular belief, diamond is not the end product of super pure coal. Diamonds were formed from the carbon atoms thrown into the primordial mix of material at the birth of our planet, over 4 billion years ago. Lighter than iron and the other elements that formed the core, carbon atoms mainly settled into what became the Earth's mid-section, or mantle. The incredible pressure and temperature experienced in that region formed the perfect crystal lattices that we now call diamond. Those mined on the surface today have been pushed upwards by the forces of deep, volcanoes.

A coal mine in Australia

Photo courtesy of Stephen Codrington, Stephen. *Planet Geography 3rd Edition* (2005) www.commons.wikimedia.org/wiki/File:Strip_coal_mining.jpg

Rock Classification

The fundamental classification system in geology is called the **Mohs Scale of Hardness**, first described way back in 1812 by Friedrich Mohs. It is a simple system, in which 10 commonly available minerals are listed from 1 to 10 in order of their relative hardness, along with their actual chemical composition:

Relative Hardness	Absolute Hardness	What It's Made Of
1- Talc	1	$Mg_3Si_4O_{10}(OH)_2$
2- Gypsum	3	$CaSO_4 \cdot 2H_2O$
3- Calcite	9	$CaCO_3$
4- Flourite	21	CaF_2
5- Apatite	48	$Ca_5(PO_4)_3(OH-,Cl-,F-)$
6- Feldspar (orthoclase)	72	$KAlSi_3O_8$
7- Quartz	100	SiO_2
8- Topaz	200	$Al_2SiO_4(OH-,F-)_2$
9- Corundum	400	Al_2O_3
10- Diamond	1600	C

Mohs scale refers to rocks, but, remember that rocks are made up of minerals. Minerals, in turn, are either pure elements, like gold or copper, or are made up of combinations of elements, like quartz (SiO_2), which is a combination of silicon and oxygen. The rock we call apatite comes in several varieties. It will always be made of calcium, phosphorus, and oxygen, but will also have one of the following: an oxygen - hydrogen group, chloride, or fluoride. The actual chemical composition of an individual piece of apatite will determine its color and other physical properties. Granite, one of the most common igneous rocks, is made up of three minerals: quartz, feldspar and mica, each of which has their own chemical composition. Anyone who has ever visited a tile store or home improvement center knows that granite comes in a myriad of colors and patterns. It is the relative proportion of each of these minerals that determines what the granite will look like. Feldspar is the grey, pink or peach colored parts of granite; the white crystals are quartz, and the shiny, black bits are mica. The unusual colors you sometimes see in decorative granite are caused by the presence of additional minerals. For example, if copper seeped into a bed of granite it would result in spots of green in the rock. Sometimes these spots are present as chunks of color, sometimes as long, serpentine stripes. These wild patterns are the visible result of all that squeezing and melting that went on under the earth millions of years ago!

The most common **element** in the Earth's crust is oxygen. In fact, oxygen makes up about 47% of the Earth's crust, although it is in the form of "oxides", meaning the oxygen is chemically bound to other elements. Silicon is the second most common element in the Earth's crust, accounting for about 28%, followed by aluminum, at about 8%, and iron at about 5%. No matter how rocks & minerals were formed, their basic composition at the molecular level is surprisingly consistent.

Everyday Activity - Play with Rocks!

Kids learn by doing and by seeing connections between what they study in school and their everyday life. Handling rocks and soil samples and classifying them based on easily identifiable characteristics like shininess, hardness, stickiness, etc. bring out the natural scientist in most kids. Many of these rock samples are cheap, easy to get (try American Science & Surplus through Amazon.com), and non-toxic, so kids can have a good time handling them and scratching their samples up. Afterwards, collect rocks from around your neighborhood and see where they fit into the scale.

A great experiment for kids is to get a collection of rocks and physically scratch one rock against another to test their relative hardness. It's fun! Talk with them about which rocks should be used for different applications. Talc is a rock that is ground up to make talcum powder – also known as baby powder. It's very, very soft. Feldspar and quartz are two of the most common minerals found in granite, which is used to make statues, buildings, and curbstones. Everyone recognizes diamond as jewelry, but industrial grade diamonds (those that can't be cut into beautiful shapes) are used to make drill bits to cut through other rocks and metals).

Pumice is a rock that floats! Sometimes, **extrusive igneous** rocks cool so quickly that lots of air gets trapped inside the lava, resulting in a loose mesh of stone with lots of air bubbles inside. Take a piece of pumice, drop it in a bowl of water and it will float. Explain to your kids how these pockets of air act the same way as the floaties they used to wear on their arms in the swimming pool. Air makes things float, whether it's trapped inside a rock or a plastic bag.

Glaciers

No understanding of geology can be complete without including the glaciers. Basic weathering affects all rocks and soil over time, but the **Ice Ages** acted on the planet with such force and over such huge areas of land that they deserve a section of their own. During the last **Ice Age**, which peaked about 20,000 years ago, most of North America was covered in ice and snow. Gargantuan sheets of ice covered all of what is now Canada and about the northern half of what is now the United States. In Europe ice sheets extended south to modern day Germany and Poland, and in Asia they extended into what is now called the Tibetan Plateau.

Glaciers are formed from the accumulation of snow. When snow falls on top of already packed snow, the snow at the bottom layers turns into ice. If this packed snow and ice doesn't melt over the summer before more snow falls the following winter, a glacier can form. Today glaciers still exist at the Earth's poles and at the tops of

Satellite image of the Malaspina Glacier in Alaska taken in 2013, courtesy of NASA

mountains, where the ambient temperature is colder than in the surrounding lowlands.

How do glaciers move? That is a question that has confounded thousands of kids (and adults, too). Every schoolchild is supposed to know that glaciers moved mountains and created valleys, but how did that actually *happen*? How can ice *move*? Glaciology is a complex science. For the purposes of this book, the actions of glaciers will be broken down into a few key points that will, hopefully, provide some insight as to the Earth - moving effects of these gigantic sheets of ice. The Ice Ages produced conditions that resulted in the accumulation of packed snow and ice over gigantic areas. When the thickness of snowpack exceeds about 150 feet, the pressure on the bottom layers is so great that its temperature increases (remember – all other things being equal, an increase in pressure leads to an increase in temperature). This increase in temperature causes the ice and snow at the bottom to melt, allowing the still-frozen ice and snow on top to slide more easily. Now imagine a glacier, at least 150 feet thick, miles long and miles wide, sliding on its bottom layer of melted water. Imagine it picking up tons (literally!) of dirt, rocks, and even boulders with it as it slides down a mountainside. That's how glaciers changed the landscape of the Earth. This type of action relocated huge amounts of rocks and dirt, carved out lake beds, and created new hills where a glacier left behind its cargo of debris.

Glaciers can also "grow" because of melting on the top layers of ice. Imagine a huge

> ## *Everyday Experiment*
> ## *Mini-glaciers 1*
>
> Take a white (snow-colored) ceramic bowl and fill it with water. Leave it in the freezer overnight. The next day, let the bowl sit in the sun for 30 minutes or so. What happens? The top layer of ice has melted, but not its sides or bottom.
>
> This melted water can slide off and roll downhill.

sheet of ice on the side of a hill. The top of the ice sheet gets warmed by the sun, but the vast middle stays frozen. The melt water on top begins to flow down a hill, spilling over the still-frozen ice underneath. As it flows down the hill, this melt water refreezes. More sun-warmed ice melts, flows, and refreezes, and so the glacier "grows", spreading downward. As this melt water flows, it's not flowing over a clean, smooth surface. Once it hits the ground, the water is surging over tons of rock, sand, dirt, etc. which get carried in its flow. When this dirty water refreezes, the rocks get frozen into it. Remember, glaciers are huge, and produce thousands of gallons of this meltwater. Over a large area and a long time, the result is that the glacier "carried" tons of rock and other debris from the top of the mountains to the bottom. One eventual result of this type of action is the **glacial moraine**, a term used to describe a field of miscellaneous rock and other debris carried by glaciers into a valley. **Eskers** are long, snakelike paths with steep sides formed when streams deposited loads of rock and dirt between ice blocks. How did this happen? When glaciers were miles high and wide, occasionally, due to changing conditions of temperature and pressure, streams of meltwater would actually form *within* the giant ice blocks. Just as today's rivers deposit silt and sediment at the bottom of their beds, these inter-glacial streams deposited layers of sediment. Over thousands of years this deposition resulted in the building up of densely packed soil and rock paths. A second way eskers formed was when meltwater, filled with sediment, flowed over the tops of glaciers. When

Esker in Einunndalsranden naturreservat, Hedmark, Norway
Courtesy of Wikipedia commons,
www.no.wikipedia.org/wiki/Fil:Esker_Einunndalen.JPG

the glaciers had crevasses present, the sediment would naturally fall into the cracks. Over time the crevasse filled with compacted dirt and rock. When the glaciers eventually receded, these molded deposits of sediment (the esker) remained. These formations are quite common, and in fact were often used as foundations for rail roads and bridges. In other cases the sand, gravel, etc. that eskers were made of was carted away and used for buildings roads elsewhere.

Other glacial landmarks we can still see today are:

- **Drumlins** - canoe-shaped hills also formed by the action of glaciers depositing debris as they moved along a large area;
- **U-shaped valleys** - formed when glaciers smoothed out the V-shaped valleys between mountains through the action of all those rocks being pushed around.
- **Erratics** – large boulders that glaciers picked up and set down in odd locations.

Everyday Experiment –
Mini-glaciers 2

Take an ice cube and let it sit at room temperature for a few minutes until its surface gets slippery. Slide it along the ground. Pick it up and observe how bits of sand, dirt, dust, etc. are now attached to the ice cube's bottom side. Now take the ice cube and slide the dirty bottom side against a clean piece of cloth, like a dishtowel. What happens? The dirt from the ground has been transferred to the clean cloth, demonstrating that ice has the ability to carry stuff from one place to another.

OK, but the little ice cube has a hand moving it around. How did gigantic ice sheets *move*? Again, some basic kitchen tools can illustrate. Take a Pyrex™ bowl and fill it with water. Place in the freezer overnight. The next day, try to move the frozen ice around. Nothing moves, right? Now place the bowl in a larger bowl of hot water so that only the bottom of the frozen bowl gets warmed. After 10 minutes or so, try sliding the ice block. It moves around easily because the ice at the bottom of the bowl has melted. Refer back to the section on Heat. Talk to your kids about what exactly is happening. When frozen, the water molecules (H_2O) are locked into a crystal lattice and can't move. Remember that heat is just a measure of molecular motion. But when they get warmed up, the little molecules start to quiver and shake, bumping up against each other and causing more molecules to move around. This is heat.

Now take this piece of ice outside and let it roll down a hill. If you don't have a hill, try kicking it across a lawn or driveway or sidewalk. Like a mini-glacier, it will pick up bits of dirt, grass, sand, etc. Now let it melt somewhere and see how all the stuff that was picked up by the ice now gets deposited where the ice melts.

Soil

Soil is actually just really finely ground rocks with some organic matter mixed in, and so, technically, a rock itself. What are all the different types of dirt made of?

- **Sand** – finely ground rocks. Beige beach sand is made of ground of rocks which contain a lot of silica (SiO_2). The bright white sand found in many tropical beaches contains lots of limestone ($CaCO_3$). Black sand is made up of finely ground basalt (of varied and complicated chemical composition), which originated from volcanic flows. The action of wind, waves, and currents over millions of years breaks down these rocks into finer and finer particles, which we call sand.

- **Clay** – this is what makes mud sticky. Clay is actually weathered feldspar, ($KAlSi_3O_8$) a component of granite. When feldspar is exposed to water over time, chemical reactions take place. One result is that the potassium (K) is replaced with water molecules (H_2O) and this change causes a relatively hard rock to become a squishy substance with very different properties.

- **Hummus** – this type of soil has a lot of organic compounds in it. In the world of chemistry, "organic" refers to chemical compounds that contain the element **carbon**. It has nothing to do with notions of purity or naturalness. Carbon is the element of life, and soil rich in organics will generally be very good for growing plants in.

Everyday Activity – Learn About Dirt!

A great activity for elementary school-aged children is to experiment with different types of soil and learn about which kinds are better suited to different purposes. Which types of soil hold water? Which types are good for growing plants? These are all great activities which are easy to set up and do at home. Get several different types of soil from different sources. Try potting soil, beach sand, compost, or whatever is available to you. Let your kids play with each sample, without mixing them up, and talk about what each sample looks and feels and smells like. Mix some soil with water and see what happens. Does the water separate out or does it combine with the soil to make mud? Now put the soil into paper or plastic cups and try planting vegetable or flower seeds in them. Which soils allow the seeds to germinate? Which ones product the healthiest plants?

Even better, use clear plastic or glass cups (washed out old jars from jelly or pickles will work fine) and plant the seeds near the sides so that they are visible. Watch as germination takes place and observe the roots moving downward and the sprouts moving up towards the surface.

Try viewing your samples with a magnifying glass or a small handheld microscope. Try **www.scientificsonline.com** for a selection of inexpensive, pocket sized tools that can magnify things up to 50 times.

LIFE SCIENCES

How Did We Get Here?

One of the most fundamental questions asked by humans throughout the ages is "How did we get here?" That is a Very Big Question. There are different ways to answer that, and the answers depend a lot on how far back in time you want to go. What is meant by "we"? Humans, primates, mammals, single cells? Let's pick up where we left off in the previous chapters on astronomy and geology.

When the Earth was formed about 4.5 billion years ago, the planet consisted of all the elements that are still here today. These elements may have been bonded with other elements in different molecular configurations, separated and re-bonded over the millennia, but the *elements* were all here. Evidence indicates that in the beginning of the planet's existence, it had a rocky surface, and molten metals formed a roiling layer under the surface rocks. Volcanic eruptions, which transported the molten rock and an array of gases up to the planet's surface, were common.

The early atmosphere was quite different from today's. One very important difference is that there was virtually no free oxygen (O_2) in the atmosphere of this infant planet. Lightning strikes happened frequently. As magma churned and lightning blazed, chemical reactions created many varied organic (carbon-containing) compounds. In warm, watery places some of these organic molecules reacted with others to form increasingly complicated molecular configurations. This environment is often referred to as the **"Primordial Soup"**, meaning a rich solution of organic compounds that somehow fostered the creation of the first true forms of Life.

Laboratory experiments done in the 1950's showed that the conditions of early Earth were capable of producing the organic molecules that are the basis of life. Stanley Miller and Harold Urey constructed a system of liquid and gaseous solutions in a series of glass bottles. The particular chemical composition of these solutions was an educated guess of what the Earth had to offer around 4 billion years ago. The solutions were heated and cooled periodically and also zapped with electric sparks to mimic lightning. Examining their solutions at the end of the experiment, Miller and Urey found that their bottles now contained many of the molecules known to be essential for life as we know it. In fact, 11 of the 20 **amino acids** had been created in this artificial primordial soup. This is not proof of how life formed, but it does provide a plausible hypothesis.

Another hypothesis is that microbial life arrived here from other planets via asteroids or comets. Note that this refers to *microbial* life, not little alien humanoids. It is plausible, and recent advances in the study of **extremophiles** (organisms that can survive in extreme conditions of hot, cold and dryness) indicate that this idea has some merit. Proof, however, is yet to come. If and when it does, learning how their genomes compare with those of various species on Earth will be very exciting! Even if further study shows that this could have happened, life did indeed originate *somewhere*. Did it happen once and then get transported around to other planets? (If so, when we have the opportunity to study extraterrestrial life forms, their genomes should be related to that of Earth-based life forms.) Or did life arise on many other planets independently? If that is the case, then learning about their genetic material, methods of reproduction and metabolism will be truly groundbreaking! Whatever we learn about the origin of life in the future, the fact remains that life did have to originate at some point, somewhere, and our earthly studies will be relevant whether that primordial soup was on Earth, on Mars, or somewhere even farther away.

EARLY LIFE

The oldest fossils of what were once living cells have been dated to the Archaean Period, about 3.6 billion years ago. These fossils are from early **Archaebacteria** - primitive, single celled creatures. The word "archaea" sounds a lot like "archaic", meaning very old, and with good reason. These tiny, primitive cells are believed to be the oldest form of life. These fossils do not look like the trilobites or dinosaur footprints that are displayed in museums. Archaebacteria were microscopic, invisible to the eye. However they left behind chemical traces that only living cells can create. When geologists determine the age of a particular rock formation, the presence of these chemical traces indicate that life forms once existed there. Archaebacteria were the initial forms of life, and so all other forms, single celled organisms, plants, animals, and, yes, humans, all evolved eventually from these tiny creatures.

The next type of life to emerge was the **Prokarya**, a form of single cell organisms that spawned most of the bacteria still present on (and vitally important to) Earth today. Along with the archaebacteria, these prokaryotic cells multiplied in number, populating the world's oceans over millions of years. Roughly 3.5 billion years ago, **cyanobacteria**, single cells with the ability to use the sun's light as a source of energy, evolved. The word "photosynthesis" means making something (synthesis) out of light (photo). These cells "made" energy for their own survival, and in doing so, expelled oxygen as a byproduct of their metabolism.

$$6\ CO_2 + 6\ H_2O \longrightarrow C_6H_{12}O_6 + 6O_2$$

This is the recipe for photosynthesis. The yellow arrow represents sunlight. The biochemical details of the process are exceedingly complex, but the overall formula is just this: in the presence of sunlight, these cells turn water and carbon dioxide into sugar and oxygen.

Some cyanobacteria grew in colonies along coastlines and in other damp areas. These colonies eventually formed mats, as successive generations of cells grew on top of the previous colonies. Sand and mineral dust stuck to the tops, and layer upon layer formed until eventually the sand and dust "cemented" the bacterial colonies into permanent mounds called stromatolites. Today, living stromatolites are extremely rare, but can be found in a few remote places.

An uncountable number of these single cells, scattered all over the Earth's oceans, photosynthesizing constantly for millions of years, *actually changed the chemical composition of the Earth's atmosphere*. Once that oxygen was in place, new and different, **aerobic** (oxygen using) forms of life began to evolve. But another change took place, which was just as profound. At first, all this newly produced O_2 was absorbed by rocks, a substantial amount by iron. Scientists today can study stratified layers of bedrock and can date an area by these layers of rust. But once the surface rock had absorbed all the O_2 it could, the oxygen gas went up into the air. There it reacted with methane gas (CH_4) which is a very potent greenhouse gas. Once in the atmosphere, the O_2 reacted with the CH_4 to form carbon dioxide, CO_2 and water.

$$2\,O_2 + CH_4 \rightarrow 2\,H_2O + CO_2$$

Stromatolites in Shark's Bay, Australia

Image courtesy of Paul Harrison, via www.commons.wikimedia.org/wiki/File:Stromatolites_in_Sharkbay.jpg

The very early Earth most likely had an atmosphere relatively high in carbon dioxide and methane, both by-products of volcanic eruptions and also of impacts of meteors crashing into the planet. Carbon Dioxide is a greenhouse gas, but a much less effective one than methane. Scientists have theorized that this global change in atmospheric conditions led to a massive change in climate, and led to the first "Snowball Earth" era. The conversion from methane (a very potent greenhouse gas) to carbon dioxide (a less effective greenhouse gas) released enough of the Earth's heat that the entire planet was covered in ice for about 300 million years.

"Greenhouse gases" are so termed because a layer of such a gas acts like a chemical greenhouse, allowing heat from the sun to penetrate inside while blocking the radiant heat from Earth from going up into space. A planet covered with an atmospheric blanket of CH_4 is kept very hot, while one covered with CO_2 is kept less warm. Still, *all other things being equal*, an atmosphere with more CO_2 warms the planet more than one with less CO_2. Mathematical comparisons between the greenhouse effects of CH_4 and CO_2 are tricky - and are the subject of active research. While CH_4 is more potent in terms of blocking radiative heat from escaping earth, it only persists in the atmosphere for about 12 years. CO_2 is less potent than CH_4, but it persists in the atmosphere for centuries. It is an undisputed fact that both gases do contribute to warming the Earth, and the presence of both in the atmosphere has increased very significantly over the past few hundred years because of human - industrial activity. This very rapid change in the atmosphere has caused, and will continue to cause, shifts in the climatic and weather patterns that we have become used to.

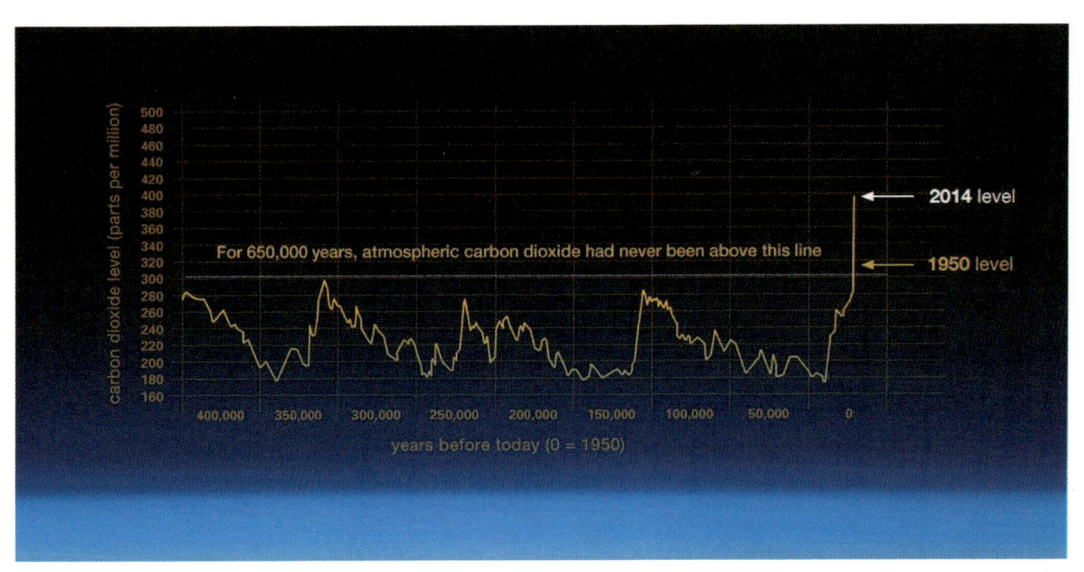

Scientists use ice core samples to reconstruct what molecules were present in the atmosphere through time. Whatever was present in the air gets trapped in ice, and so by digging into geologic formations of known ages, they can determine what gases were present through time.

Image courtesy of www.climate.nasa.gov/evidence/

More complex **eukaryotic organisms** appeared about 2 billion years ago. The first eukaryotes were single celled algae. Scientists think that **plant cells** may have begun when a larger cell engulfed a cyanobacterial cell. Instead of being killed, the smaller cell adapted to living inside, and became a functioning part of the larger cell. The large cell offered protection from the environment, and the small cell, in turn, gave the products of its own photosynthesis to the large cell. These enclosed smaller cells could have been the first **chloroplasts**. Likewise, **mitochondria** may also have begun as engulfed smaller cells which became functioning parts of larger cells.

The earliest **multicellular** organisms evolved approximately 600 million years ago. Perhaps what started with microbial clumping together, cells forming colonies in the shape of mats and filaments, progressed into different parts of the colony specializing in different tasks. Gradually, some individual cells became more efficient at consuming food while others developed a more durable cell wall to protect against the elements. Over time, each individual cell became more and more dependent upon its fellow colony-mates, as they essentially shared their skills. It's easy to imagine this happening concurrently, increased **symbiosis** (a mutually advantageous relationship) happening among a countless number of different cell types and gradually leading to many different types of early eukaryotic life.

About 500 million years ago, in what is now called the early **Paleozoic Era**, the first land based plants started to grow. Until this point all life existed in wet or damp environments. Once survival on land became possible, these new plants also contributed to the addition of O_2 to the Earth's atmosphere. The next 300 million years produced an explosion of new forms of life. Beginning with trilobites, corals and shellfish and culminating in flying and crawling insects, reptiles and amphibians, spiders, trees, and ferns, life experienced an incredible growth spurt.

The **Triassic** (about 250 million years ago) **Jurassic** (about 200 million years ago), **and Cretaceous** (about 150 million years ago) periods saw the evolution of the dinosaurs, and lots of other things too. Not only the familiar Tyrannosaurus and Stegosaurus, but birds with feathers, mammals, bees and butterflies, and flowering plants all emerged and thrived during these epochs.

Throughout these 3.6 billion years of evolving Life, five **mass extinctions** occurred, each one eliminating many of the major species on Earth at that time. They came at approximately the following times:

> 440 million years ago
> 360 Million years ago
> 250 million years ago*
> 200 million years ago
> 65 million years ago

The Permian Extinction (250 million years ago*) is estimated by scientists to be the most devastating - approximately 96% of all life present on Earth at that time is believed to have been wiped out in a relatively short period of time. That means that all subsequent forms of living creatures were descended from the 4% that survived the Permian event. The most recent extinction, around 65 million years ago, famously killed off the dinosaurs, along with many other animals and plant forms. Yet, each of these extinction periods had a silver lining: New forms of life were able to thrive in the new environmental conditions caused by the extinction event. The lack of dinosaurs and other large, carnivorous reptiles cleared the way for mammals to thrive on this transformed land. Pigs, dogs, bears, and early primates populated landmasses that produced flowering plants and grasses. The oceans teemed with everything from mollusks to whales. Most of the life forms we have on Earth today can be traced back through time to these beginnings, approximately 60 million years ago.

It's important to realize that this process is constant. The time of a human life or even several generations of human life is so small as compared to the history of Life, that the current state of affairs seems fixed and unchanging. But it is not and never has been. Recent recognition that the Earth is currently experiencing a sixth massive extinction is very humbling, considering this background information, and the likelihood that humans are causing it. Historical evidence suggests that the Earth will come out of this just fine, and even that other forms of life will adapt and flourish in the new conditions. But this process will take millions of years.

Everyday Activity
Digital Archaeology

If your kids are particularly interested in learning more about our distant past there are many great sources of information. There are even more sources that are not very accurate, so search and read with a healthy dose of skepticism. Here are a few that are very trustworthy and fun:

http://www.sdnhm.org/kids/dinosaur/

http://paleobiology.si.edu

http://www.bbc.co.uk/nature/history_of_the_earth

http://www.nhm.ac.uk/jdsml/nature-online/dino-directory/

http://www.paleoportal.org/

http://www.pbs.org/wgbh/evolution/extinction/dinosaurs/index.html

What Is Life?

How can scientists define the beginning of life? What was the difference between a bunch of complex molecules floating around in the primordial muck and the first actual living cells? What exactly defines "Life"?

Classification of life vs. non-life is can be very frustrating. Usually these answers are obvious, sometimes they seem obvious but aren't, and once in a while the answers can be downright confusing. For example, if one had to classify a pebble as "life" or "non-life", the answer would easily be "non-life". But what about an acorn? It looks like a pebble, and feels like a pebble, but it meets the criteria of "live". Likewise, a tree is clearly "live" but what about a branch of the tree that has been cut off?

Since the time of the ancient Greeks, philosophers have debated the definition of life, and most scientists still do, but there is general agreement on a set of criteria. At a simple level, in order to be considered "alive" something has to have these three qualities:

- **A metabolism - the ability to take in some sort of fuel and expel waste products**
- **A barrier between itself and the outside world coupled with the ability to respond to stimuli from the outside world**
- **The ability to replicate / reproduce**

Going back to the description of the origination of Life on Earth, no one knows the exact moment that a collection of molecules came together in such a way that they, quite literally, took on a life of their own. But at some point, the first cells formed in that primordial soup accomplished three things:

1) Organic compounds clustered together in such a way that they consumed other chemicals and expelled what they didn't need (metabolism),

2) They separated and protected themselves from the outside world (environmental response), and

3) They managed to replicate themselves, creating offspring that were identical to themselves (reproduction).

Bacteria are tiny, living cells that are invisible to human eyes. They exist as individual cells and each cell is enclosed in its own wall. Each individual cell can respond to stimuli from the environment and consumes food and expels waste. Each cell has the ability to reproduce asexually, by dividing itself into two identical clones. Bacteria are most definitely alive.

Viruses are particles of genetic material packed into a protein shell. Think of an M&M with its candy coating surrounding all the chocolate-y goodness. Viruses are very, very good at reproducing themselves, yet viruses are generally considered to be non-life. They are essentially strands of self-replicating genetic material, either DNA or RNA, held together by a protein coating, but viruses cannot metabolize anything. They are inactive until they take over a host cell and then they use the host cell's biologic machinery to build new virus particles.

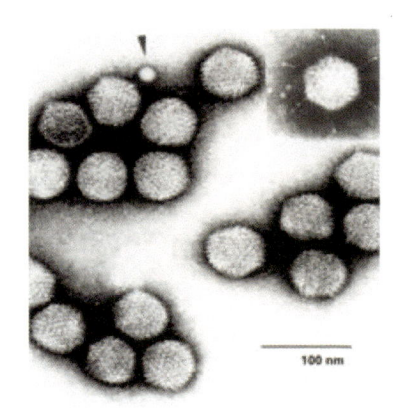

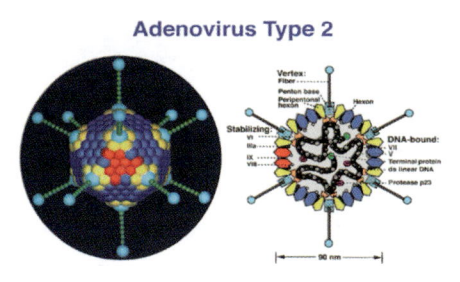

An electron micrograph of actual adenovirus and a scientific model of the same.

Adenovirus are responsible for many common infections in humans and animals.

www.microbiology2009.wikispaces.com/Adenovirus+Use+in+Gene+Therapy+and+Vaccines

A Very Brief Introduction to Cell Biology

To understand the differences between, let's say, bacterial and human cells, an understanding of basic cell biology is helpful. In elementary school kids learn that living things are made of cells, but they typically learn what those cells are made of when they are a lot older. Nevertheless, as parents, it's good to stay one step ahead. The first thing to understand is that there are different kinds of cells.

Prokaryotic cells are simple cells. All prokaryotic organisms exist only as single celled creatures. These cells are wrapped in a **cell wall** that acts as a barrier between the cell and the outside world. Inside the cell wall resides its DNA and various proteins that help the cell to function.

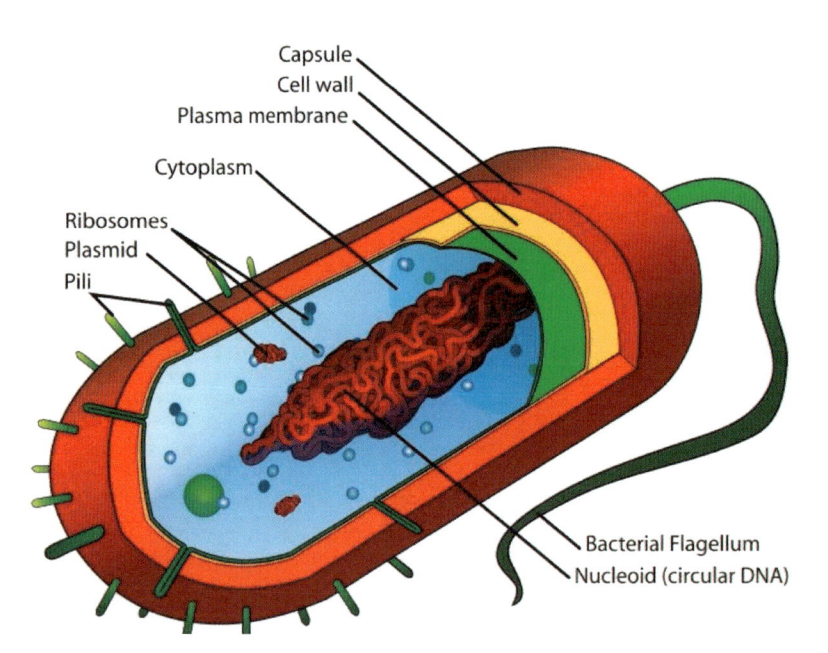

Prokaryotic Cell Courtesy of Mariana Ruiz, www.commons.wikipedia.org

Eukaryotic cells are much more complex and also much larger than prokaryotes. Some eukaryotes exist as single-celled organisms (e.g. yeast), but all **multicellular organisms** (e.g. humans) are made of eukaryotic cells. Inside every eukaryotic cell are structures called **organelles**. These are highly specialized units, each of which has a distinct role in the cell's overall life. A few examples of the most important organelles are listed below:

> **Mitochondria** - the "engines" of the cell. Chemical reactions that happen inside these organelles provide the energy for the cell to live and carry on its other functions.
>
> **Nucleus** – the "design center" of the cell. The nucleus is where the DNA is, and the DNA provides the "blueprints" of how the cell is constructed.
>
> **Smooth Endoplasmic Reticulum** – the "factories" of the cell. Various chemical components are transported into the ER and processed to be useful to the rest of the cell. In the smooth ER, fat molecules are often processed for use elsewhere in the cell.
>
> **Rough Endoplasmic Reticulum** – more "factories". This ER appears rough when observed under a microscope because tiny **ribosomes** are attached to it. These ribosomes are the sites on which RNA gets matched up with amino acids to start the protein making process.
>
> **Golgi Apparatus** – the "shipping department". Once molecules are made in the smooth and rough ER they get transported to this organelle for final packaging and shipping to the areas in which they are needed.
>
> **Lysosomes** – the "custodians" of the cell. These bubbles contain the enzyme lysozyme, which destroys waste products from the cell and prepares them to be sent out.
>
> **Cytoplasm** – All the organelles inside a cell are suspended in this thick liquid, kind of like chocolate chips swirled through vanilla pudding.

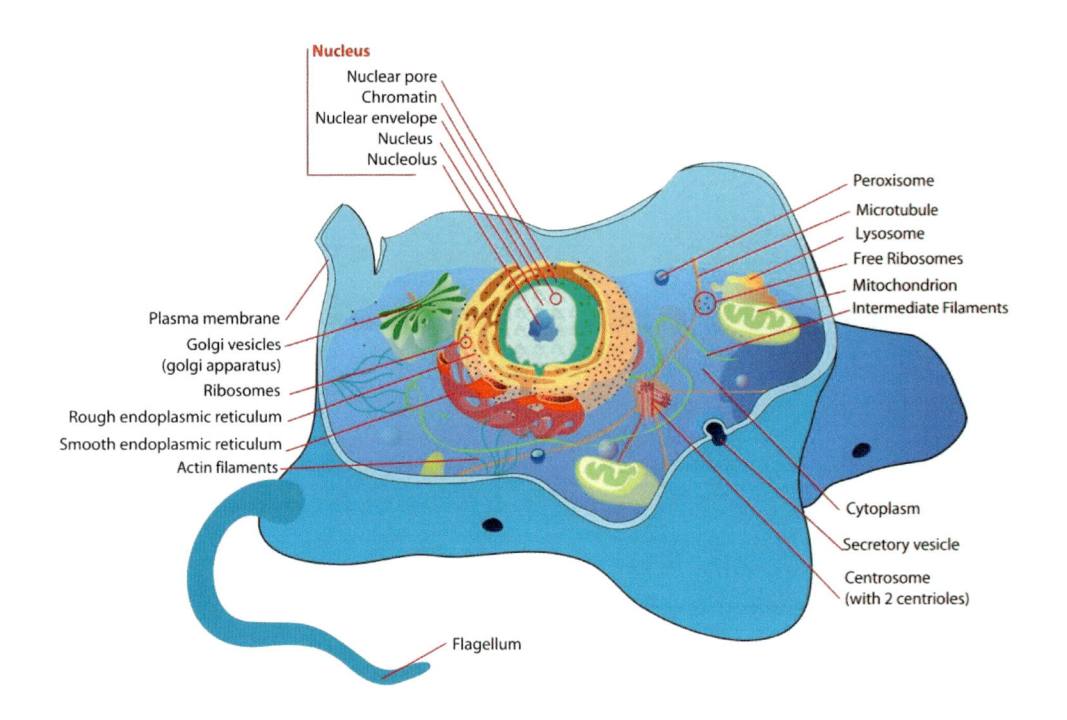

Drawing of simplified animal cell
courtesy of Mariana Ruiz via
www.en.wikipedia.org/wiki/File:Animal_cell_structure_en.svg

A Very Brief Introduction to Molecular biology

One of the three requirements for "Life" is the ability to reproduce. Offspring are supposed to be identical (in the case of single cells splitting into two separate "daughter" cells) or similar (in the case of sexual reproduction) to their parents. In either case, the molecule required for reproduction is the same: Deoxyribonucleic acid, commonly known as **DNA**, is the molecule that stores genetic information. This information is grouped into units we call **genes**. In addition to genes themselves, many segments of DNA code for instructions on what to do with certain genes: turn them off, enhance their function, multiply their number, delay their activity, etc. Many, many genes and instruction codes are strung together to form the length of a DNA molecule, and these are organized into specific, self-contained structures called **chromosomes**. The number of chromosomes present in a particular cell is a defining characteristic of each species.

DNA is comprised of carbon, hydrogen, oxygen, nitrogen, and phosphorous. The "deoxyribose" part of deoxyribonucleic acid refers to sugar molecules that make up the backbone of the DNA molecule. The genetic information of DNA is defined by the sequence of four particular, and very important, molecules called **bases**: **Adenine (A), Thymine (T), Cytosine (C) and Guanine (G)**. Each of these molecules contains carbon, hydrogen, nitrogen and oxygen bonded together in a particular configuration. In the picture below, each angle represents a single atom of carbon.

The sequence in which the A's, C's, G's, and T's are strung together define an organism's genetic makeup. Very small changes can make huge differences. The

How the base pairs of DNA bond

Image courtesy of Wikipedia www.commons.wikimedia.org/wiki/File:AT-GC.jpg

difference in the sequence between human and chimpanzee DNA is only about 1.2%. So 98.8% of our DNA is the same as that of a chimp. Even more awesome is that about 60% of a human being's DNA is the same as the DNA of a banana plant. In this case, the remaining 40% makes an awful lot of difference.

> **Review the section on Chemistry:**
>
> Hydrogen was created during the Big Bang and Carbon, Oxygen and Phosphorous were all created during star formation, exploded during a supernova, and coalesced into our planet. Every atom that makes up every molecule of DNA shares this history.

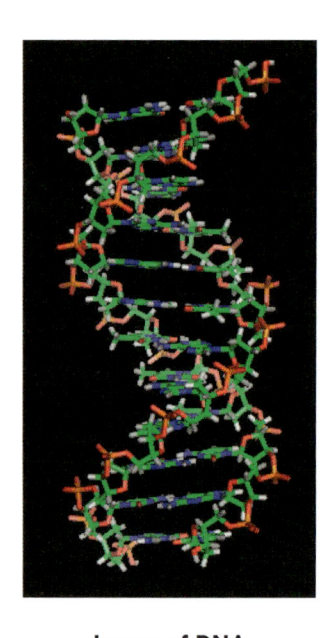

Image of DNA

The different colors represent acual molecules (A-T; C-G) that connect across to each other and form the 3-dimensional structure.

Image courtesy of Tim Vickers via www.commons.wikimedia.org

Across all forms of life, whether they are plankton floating in the ocean, grasses in the savannah, or in the cells of your own body, in the double helix structure, Adenine (A) only pairs up with Thymine (T) and Cytosine (C) only pairs with Guanine (G). This is because, at a chemical level, these molecules' shapes fit very well together.

The DNA molecule itself has been compared to many things, (a twisted ladder, a zipper, a photocopy machine, or a set of blueprints) and all with good reasons:

The atoms of the DNA molecule join together in an intricate three-dimensional structure that looks, sort of, like a **ladder** that has been twisted from top to bottom. This three-dimensional structure is called a **double helix**.

The **zipper** comparison is based on the way that DNA works. Various enzymes (molecules made of protein) grab on to this double helix and untwist it, exposing the two halves of the ladder, just the way a zipper pull separates the two halves of a zipper. Once its center rungs are exposed, two different things can happen:

During **mitosis** (described below) DNA acts as its own **photocopy machine**. Once the double helix is separated into its two halves, enzymes specific to the replication (doubling) process copy each half of the DNA molecule, producing two sets of identical DNA molecules. On the half where an adenine is exposed, enzymes add a new thymine to it. Where a thymine is exposed, enzymes add a new adenine to it, and so also for cytosine and guanine. Newly constructed sugar and phosphate molecules are brought together to create new backbones too, resulting in two complete, identical DNA molecules where there was originally only one. After being copied, the both new DNA molecules form into the double helix structure again.

During **transcription**, the DNA molecule serves as a **blueprint** for the next step in the process. Enzymes specific to the transcription process also untwist and unzip the double helix and expose its center rungs, but these enzymes copy the DNA halves using slightly different molecules. In this case, adenine gets matched with a molecule called **uracil** (U) instead of thymine. This process results in the original molecule of DNA (reconnected and back in its double helix) plus a single stranded molecule of **messenger ribonucleic acid**, or **mRNA**. The information encoded in the mRNA now will get **translated** into a series of amino acids.

Amino acids get synthesized and strung along like beads on a necklace, based on the instructions encoded on the mRNA. When the correct number of these amino acid "beads" is in place, they will be folded into three dimensional structures, like tying a necklace into a knot. This is how proteins are formed.

Comparison of DNA and mRNA

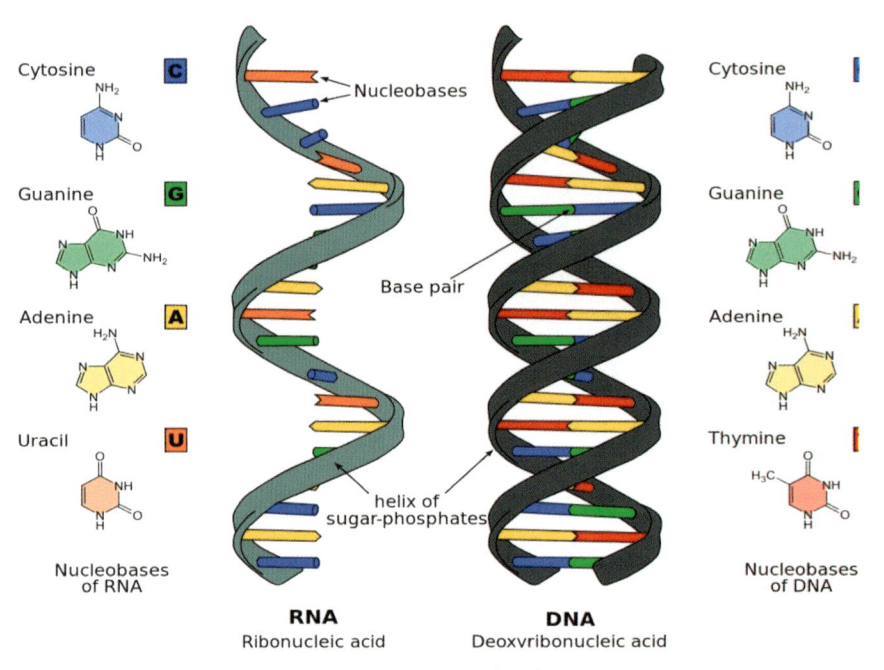

Image courtesy of www.commons.wikimedia.org/wiki/File:Difference_DNA_RNA-EN.svg

The processes described above are so universal that they are collectively known as the "Central Dogma" of biology.

DNA → RNA → Amino Acids → Protein

DNA holds the genetic blueprints for each individual organism, whether the organism is an amoeba, a maple tree or a human being. This genetic information is transcribed into mRNA which is translated into amino acids and these amino acids are folded into protein. Protein molecules perform almost all the functions of cells. While this very brief description provides a rudimentary summary of genetics, please keep in mind that it does not even scratch the surface of the amazing and intricate complexity of the whole process.

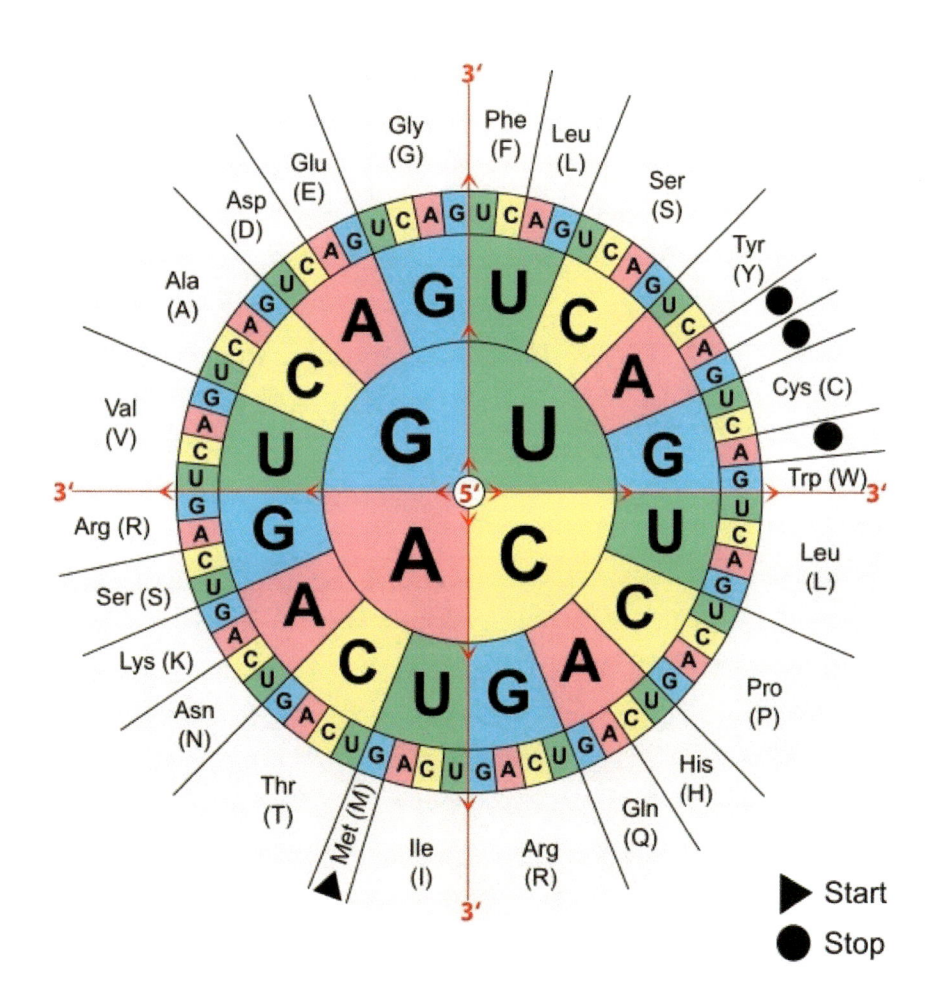

This image beautifully illustrates the entire genetic code.

Read from the inside (5') towards the outside (3') direction. For example, the messenger RNA sequences CUU, CUC, CUA and CUG will dictate the insertion of the amino acid leucine into the amino acid sequence. The mRNA sequence AUG dictates the start of a new gene sequence and UGA, UAA and UAG all dictate the stop of a particular gene sequence.

Image courtesy of Wikipedia Commons
www.commons.wikimedia.org/wiki/File:Aminoacids_table.svg

Examples of two amino acid molecules, guanine (left) and tyrosine (right)
The letters C, O, N and H refer to carbon, oxygen, hydrogen, nitrogen and hydrogen atoms, respectively. Every unmarked angle represents a single carbon atom as well. Single lines represent single bonds between the atoms and double lines represent double bonds.

Division = Multiplication

Both prokaryotic and eukaryotic cells reproduce through cell division, producing two identical "daughter" cells from a single parent cell. In prokaryotes, the chromosome is typically a simple, circular entity, but in eukaryotes the DNA exists as linear structures called **chromosomes** that reside within the cell's nucleus. Thanks to sexual reproduction, each cell has two versions of each chromosome. Different species have different numbers of chromosomes; humans have 23 pairs. Chromosomes are accompanied by proteins and RNA that give it structure and regulate its function; this DNA-RNA-protein complex is called **chromatin**. Most of the time the chromosomes exist in a relatively loose, unfolded state, that is invisible in the microscope, and it is in this state that DNA replication takes place.

The process of cell division (cell doubling) is called **mitosis**. Some of the highlights of mitosis are as follows: Once DNA replication has taken place (each chromosome has been duplicated) the chromatin condenses into distinct structures easily visible in the microscope. In humans there are now 92 chromosomes, two times 23 pairs. Then one set of each chromosome pair goes to one side of the nucleus and the other, identical chromosome pair goes to the other side. The nucleus itself then pulls apart, separating into two new nuclei, each with an identical copy of the original DNA. The entire cell then pulls apart, in a process called **cytokinesis** (cyto- cell; kinesis - movement) with a nucleus in each new daughter cell. The two resulting cells are **clones** of the original cell, meaning that an identical copy of each of the chromosomes and the genes that they contain is now possessed by each of the daughter cells.

There is a special, subsequent process that takes place in the reproductive cells of eukaryotic cells. The reproductive cells of both plants and animals (in humans these would be the female's eggs and the males' sperm) undergo a process called **meiosis**. In most eukaryotes, all cells exist with the chromosomes in duplicate form, meaning each strand of genetic material is attached to a copy of itself. In the cells destined for reproductive use, once a cell divides, it goes a step further so that four cells are produced from one. Each of these four contains a single copy of each chromosome, instead of the normal pair. A cell with a single copy of each chromosome is called "**haploid**", and the special cells with single copies of each chromosome are called **gametes**. When

> *Everyday Activity - Visualizing Mitosis & Meiosis*
>
> Watching video of stylized chromosomes go through these processes can be very helpful, but beware! There are many available that are too simplistic, too complicated or just boring. Search for videos from trustworthy sites. Public Television (PBS.org) offers excellent videos on scientific subjects. Generally those with a .edu or .gov address are legitimate. Be wary of videos uploaded by students for their own biology projects! Those can sometimes be full of all sorts of mis-information.

mating occurs, a male gamete (the sperm) containing the full set of single chromosomes from the father combines with (fertilizes) a female gamete (the egg) containing the full set of single chromosomes from the mother. (This is one reason that mating can only occur between members of the same species. Different species have too many differences in their chromosomes for proper matching up to occur.) Since they are not identical, some genes from the mother will dominate for a certain trait, and some genes from the father will dominate for another trait. The newly created offspring will, therefore, have some genetic information from the mother, and some from the father, but be a unique individual.

Mitosis   **Meiosis**

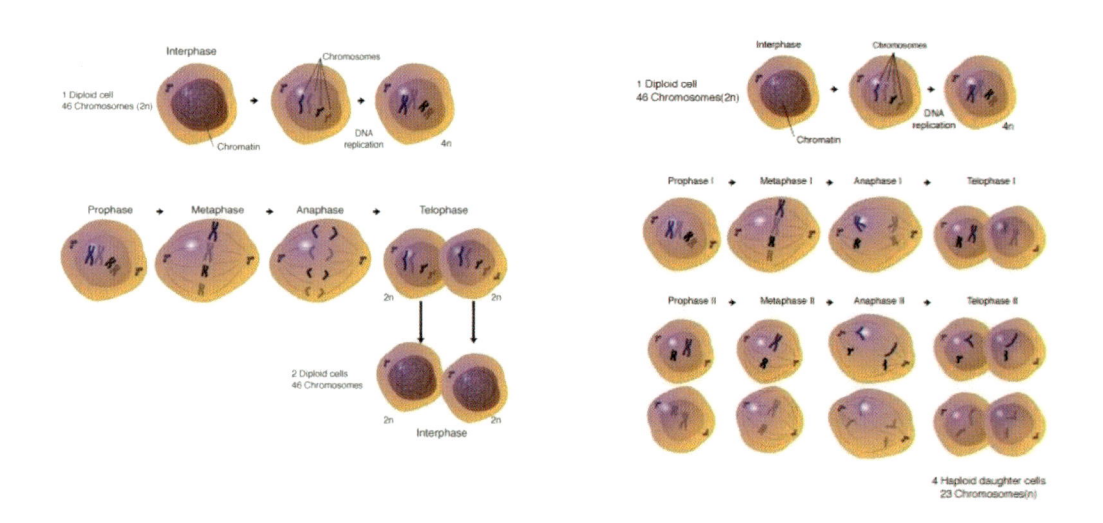

Illustrations of mitosis, left and meiosis, right

courtesy of www.ghr.nlm.nih.gov/handbook/howgeneswork/cellsdivide

INHERITANCE & GENE EXPRESSION

"Genetics", and, in particular, "molecular genetics", is the study of what happens at a *chemical* level when DNA gets transcribed and translated. At a chemical level it is vastly complex, and still only partially understood. Genes are turned on, turned off, enhanced and diminished by a variety of chemicals, some produced by the cell itself and others introduced from the environment.

Pea plant, *pisum satvium*

Image courtesy of
www.en.wikipedia.org/wiki/File:Doperwt_
rijserwt_peulen_Pisum_sativum.jpg

"Inheritance" refers to the actual passing on of traits from parent to offspring on a more holistic level. A century before Watson, Crick and Franklin discovered the structure of the DNA molecule, Gregor Mendel was figuring out the idea of inherited traits. He methodically bred pea plants for many years, following each generation and recording noticeable features of these plants, such as flower color, in order to figure out some kind of pattern to inheritance. In doing so he discovered one of the central principles of genetics.

Mendel proposed the idea of dominant and recessive genes, that only the **dominant** traits will be expressed in the offspring. Mendel realized that the **recessive** traits are still there, but they are just hidden. His mathematical calculations can be easily demonstrated with a little matrix, called a Punnett Square. These are usually popular activities in middle school biology classes. A plant or animal cell has two copies of each gene in its **genotype**, one from its mother and the other from its father (thanks to the process of meiosis, described above).

Let's say you have a female guinea pig with short hair and a male guinea pig with long hair. We will call the short haired gene **sh** and the long haired gene **LH**. Let's say that the long hair gene is dominant over the short hair gene, meaning that if both **LH** and **sh** copies of the gene are present, the baby guinea pig will be long haired. Since long hair is dominant, any short haired guinea pig *must* have two copies of the short hair gene, so its genotype is **sh sh**. We call this genotype **homozygous**, meaning that the guinea pig carries two copies of the same form of the gene. *(in scientific words, the prefix homo = same)* A long haired guinea pig could have two copies of the gene for long hair, so its genotype could be homozygous **LH LH**. But, since the log haired gene is dominant, this long haired guinea pig could also have a genotype of **LH sh**. In this case we say that this guinea pig is **heterozygous** *(in scientific words, the prefix hetero = different)*. Let's use an example of a homozygous, short haired mother (**sh sh**) and a homozygous long haired father (**LH LH**).

Mother → ↓ Father	sh	sh
LH	LH sh	LH sh
LH	LH sh	LH sh

In this case, every child will inherit one sh gene and one **LH** gene, and so every child will be long haired. The traits actually exhibited by an organism are called its **phenotype**. In this Punnett Square, all offspring have the long-haired phenotype, because they will all have long hair, although their genotypes contain both **LH** and **sh** genes.

It gets more interesting as you go through more generations. Let's say one of these boy baby guinea pigs (**LH sh**) grows up and mates with a long haired girl guinea pig from a different family. Let's also say that that this girl guinea pig is also heterozygous for long hair, (**LH sh**).

Mother → ↓ Father	**LH**	**sh**
LH	LH LH	LH sh
sh	LH sh	sh sh

Look what happens! Three of these guinea pigs exhibit long hair, just like their parents. But one of these four has two copies of the recessive **sh sh** gene, and so will have short hair. It will look more like one of its grandparents. In humans, for example, a red-headed child can be born from two dark-haired parents, even though dark hair is dominant. If the child has a grandparent on both the maternal and paternal sides that had red hair, that gene has been passed down through the generations even though it is not exhibited by either parent.

Of course, in reality there is no guarantee that if four guinea pigs are born, three will have long hair and one will have short hair. Rather, *each square represents a mathematical probability that these outcomes will occur.* In other words, in the example above each individual guinea pig child has a 25% chance of being born with short hair and each individual child has a 75% chance of being born with long hair. But each child has its own chances. Sometimes all four children could have either long or short hair. Over an entire population, however, these percentages are likely to be accurate.

This explanation only holds true for genes where there is a clear dominant and recessive version. However, like so many other things in science, there are many complexities and exceptions to the rule. Some genes are co-dominant, meaning they share dominance; some genes' function is to turn other genes on or off, or to magnify or reduce their activity. Some traits are the products of many genes which independently vary, making inheritance all but impossible to predict from simple genetics.

Today we know that genetics and inheritance are inextricably linked. Scientists who study molecular genetics can see the results of their experiments in real life, whether they study mice or fruit flies or soybeans. Scientists who work in zoology or agriculture can look to the genetics of their subjects to answer a range of questions, ranging from what they will look like to how well they can tolerate drought. Human traits, from susceptibility to disease to behavioral characteristics are increasingly being defined in terms of genetics.

How Changes Happen

With every new generation there is the potential for something to change. Under perfect conditions:

> A prokaryotic cell will divide into two daughter cells which are clones (identical copies) of the mother;

> And an egg and a sperm from a female and male organism will fuse together, creating offspring that have some genetic information from each of the two parents.

However, every time cells divide, there is a chance that some tiny piece or pieces of the parent DNA — its hereditary information — will get copied incorrectly. An incorrect base may be inserted during transcription. Some small segment of DNA may be duplicated or removed entirely. **These are genetic mutations.**

In general, differences that allow improvement in the organism's life are perpetuated throughout the population over time, and those that disadvantage an organism will likely disappear from the population. Helpful mutations may confer greater strength,

> The Human Genome contains about 3×10^9 base pairs - those matched pairs of A's, T's, C's, and G's explained earlier in the chapter. That is 3,000,000,000 pairs. In any of these pairs, mistakes can happen during replication (copying of DNA during mitosis) or in translation (copying DNA into mRNA). Sometimes one base is simply left out, or an additional one is inserted. Other mistakes involve a substitution of the wrong base. Obviously, deletion or insertion mutations would mess up the sequence of amino acids, and so are more serious. Substitution of one base pair for another, however, can potentially lead to new and interesting characteristics.

speed, agility, or ability to withstand colder (or warmer) temperatures. They may confer the ability to digest foods that others in the community cannot. Mutations may bestow sharper eyesight, a keener sense of smell, or higher intelligence. Any of these traits would increase an individual organism's ability to live longer, eat more food, reproduce more, and hence, pass on this mutation to more and more future members of its community. Mutations that cause a disadvantage to an organism have the opposite effect, and these individuals do not live as long or reproduce as successfully as their competitors, and so these mutations do not get passed along through their descendants.

But there is randomness at play. Uncountable positive mutations may have occurred over time, yet that individual organism was killed for some unrelated reason, before

> Sickle cell anemia is a disease caused by a genetic mutation that results in red blood cells being misshapen. Individuals that are heterozygous (1 copy of a normal gene and 1 copy of the sickle cell gene) are better able to resist malarial infection. In environments where malaria-carrying mosquitoes are endemic, this mutation confers an obvious advantage. However, in environments where malaria is not a problem, there is no advantage to be had. There is a significant disadvantage, in that carriers of the gene run the risk of passing the mutated gene on to their children, and, if both parents are carriers, then each child would have a 25% chance of being homozygous for sickle cell, and therefore, would face a difficult life. Sickle cell blood cells do not live as long as normal blood cells and they cannot carry oxygen, and people who carry two copies of the sickle cell gene suffer from chronic fatigue and pain. From an evolutionary standpoint, it is beneficial to run the risk of some individuals being cursed with this disease, in order to confer resistance a larger percentage of the population. Those with only one copy (heterozygotes) generally are symptom free, and can lead a normal life.

it had a chance to reproduce, and the mutation was lost. There are also examples of mutations which confer an advantage to the organism in one environment, yet are disadvantageous when the organism moves to a different environment or if their native environment changes. Some mutations may be neutral, offer no real benefits or disadvantages, and so can perpetuate through a population without any effect on the community's overall well being. Some mutations have a negative impact on the organism's chances at survival, yet sometimes these individuals manage to survive and produce offspring, despite their mutation.

A series of mutations could eventually lead to the development of a completely different species. Over millions of years, an uncountable number of these mutations occurred, resulting in the huge variety of life on Earth. Mutations happen naturally and go on constantly, in every environment on the planet. Of course, traits that are

> **Epigenetics** is a branch of genetics that explores the ways that environmental conditions can affect the genetic profile of an individual independent of their actual DNA sequence. Such conditions can include chronic exposure to chemicals or long term, repetitive physical activity or emotional stress. Cells respond to environmental conditions by adapting on a biochemical level, and this adaptation sometimes involves the modification of DNA by attaching small molecules to the DNA. The purpose of these small molecules is to turn certain genes on or off, or to magnify or reduce a particular gene's overall activity. Although the actual genetic code - the sequence of bases - is unchanged, these epigenetic alternations should help the individual cope with the environmental stressors.
>
> Very recent research has shown that the epigenetic factors not only play a part in modifying an individual's overall phenotype, but may also get passed on to offspring, and become embedded in the genealogy for future generations.

"better" in one situation are not necessarily better universally. Some traits may benefit creatures living in very cold environments, for example while other would benefit creatures living in tropical conditions. Over time, things tend to sort themselves out. Today we see populations that seem to be perfectly suited to their environments: giraffes with long necks, zebras with stripes, insects that look exactly like the leaves they eat. But giraffes never "decided" to grow longer necks. Rather, bit by bit, incremental changes in neck size in some leaf-eating mammal occurred, and these longer necked versions got to eat more food. (Since many animals could reach the low-hanging leaves, those with longer necks could reach a source of food that their competitors could not, hence they got stronger. At some times, this ability may have meant the difference between getting a sufficient supply of nutrients and starving to death.) Over eons of time a specific type of animal with a very long neck evolved. Likewise the giraffe's spotted fur evolved concurrently, but independently. The spots served as camouflage in the African grasslands, reducing a spotted individual's likelihood of being seen sand eaten by a hungry carnivore.

An interesting and inadvertent experiment occurred in England during the early years of the Industrial Revolution. Most moths of the species *Biston betularia* were colored a light, speckled grey, but there was some natural genetic diversity so that in the entire population there were also some darker gray and black moths too. These moths spend most of their time attached to the sides of trees that are covered with grayish lichens, hence, under normal conditions the speckled ones were easily camouflaged by their surroundings and therefore evaded predators more successfully than their darker cousins. However, when factories started spewing soot into the London air, the barks of trees became darker, sootier versions of their former selves. The lighter, speckled grey moths were no longer easily camouflaged, but rather stood out quite starkly, while the darker moths were difficult for predators to see against the sooty background.

Within about 40 years, the percentage of speckled moths in London went down dramatically and the percentage of darker moths went up, thus providing an example of very quick evolutionary adaptation of a community. During this time, moths that lived in the unpolluted countryside experienced no such changes in the overall coloration of the community.

The peppered moth - *Biston betularia f. typical* and *Biston betularia f. carbonaria*

Photos courtesy of Olaf Leillinger via
http://en.wikipedia.org/wiki/Peppered_moth_evolution

Probably nothing has been more contested in the recent history of science than the concept of a species evolving from something considered lesser than itself. Since 1859 when Charles Darwin published his singularly famous work, *On the Origin of Species,* controversy over this subject has ebbed and flowed, but never really gone away. Typically this controversy focuses on the evolution of humans. Some people have a hard time reconciling the perceived inconsistencies between humans gradually descending from other primates, and their religious ideals of humans being designed from scratch in the image of some Greater Being. It is important to remember that **evolution is not linear, in it branching.** Humans and gorillas and chimps *do* have common ancestors, if you go back millions of years. If you go back even farther, we share common ancestors with all animals and with all eukaryotic organisms.

The principle of evolution fits consistently with every other known scientific paradigm. Everything else, from the changes in moths' wing color to the differences between modern wheat and wild type grasses, to the genetic basis of cancer, fits into the theory of evolution. In fact, very recent advances in biology continue to add proof to Darwin's theories. How could it be any other way? Consider the morphological and biochemical similarities between animals of all sorts. Lemurs and llamas, penguins and porcupines, komodo dragons and koalas, humans and hippopotami, all have eyes that see, hearts that beat, lungs that exchange oxygen for carbon dioxide, and an immune system that fights off invaders.

Modern genetic analysis techniques allow us to quantify the comparisons between humans and our closest primate relatives. Consider the genetic composition of humans, gorillas, and chimpanzees. We now know that humans and gorillas share only about 98.0% of DNA sequencing, while humans and chimps share approximately 98.8% of the genetic blueprint, and the genetic match between random pairs of human beings is over 99.9%.

What we witness today is a snapshot of the march of biological time. Organisms are continually changing bit by bit, and when mutations occur that offer significant advantages, they, too, will eventually become part of the populations of the future. This is simply genetics at work, randomly shuffling and sorting out species into their home ecosystems.

Development in Animals

In biology, the word development refers to all of the changes that take place between the merging of an egg and a sperm into a **zygote**, and the maturation of that being into an adult. The period of **gestation** (conception to birth) is a big part of that, but the early part of an organism's life can also see many changes. Development in a moth, for example, is extremely different from development of a human, yet, throughout the animal kingdom, the similarities between species are even more striking than are the differences.

Animals breed sexually, meaning that genetic information from a mother and a father is combined to form offspring with traits from both parents. This comingling of DNA gives the offspring the chance to develop with the "better" versions of each gene, because having two versions of each gene allows for the one of the two to dominate (remember Punnett Squares?). Such comingling is also extremely beneficial to the species as a whole. Over time this results in a community that is increasingly optimized for survival in its native environment. Once those male and female gametes combine, and their genetic information is shared, wonderful things start to happen.

Human Fertilization

Once a sperm fertilizes an egg, creating a zygote, changes occur that result in the implantation of an embryo in the uterine wall.

Image courtesy of Ttrue12, via www.en.wikipedia.org/wiki/File:Human_Fertilization.png

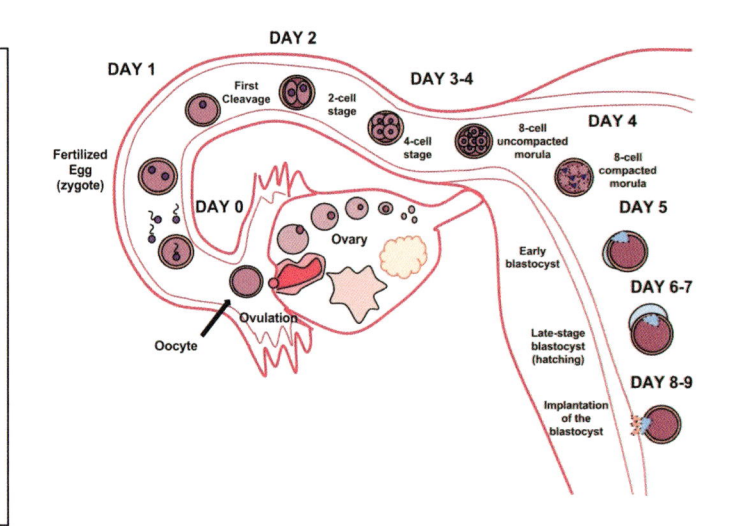

In humans, over the course of nine months, a human being is formed from a single cell, the fertilized egg, into a complete baby. Other creatures have different gestation times, but the overall process is the same: a single cell develops into a complete organism. How do the individual cells that make up all our organs - the brain, limbs, skin, immune cells, etc., know where to go and how to grow? These processes are controlled by a complex and only partially understood set of processes. One type of molecule known to influences this process are the **transcription factors**, which "tell" each cell or group of cells what they will become and what they must do to achieve their destiny. In the earliest stages of embryonic development, all cells have the ability to become any type of cell. Think about it - each fertilized egg has the organism's entire genome within itself, right? During the first few cell divisions, each daughter cell is **pluripotent**, pluri- (many) potent (as in potential). As development proceeds each cell must follow instructions provided by a series of chemical messengers, very complex molecules that cause certain genes to be turned on and others to be turned off. The result is that future epidermal cells, for example, retain their ability to become skin, hair follicles, sweat glands, etc., but lose their ability to act as heart cells. Likewise, future nerve cells are turning on the genes that control sight, hearing, emotion and thought, and lose their ability to, for example, create urine. Throughout the gestational period uncountable changes like these take place, with further refinements and improvements to the organism's development with each passing day.

As development proceeds, specific groups of cells become tissues, which coalesce into functional groups called organs, and organs with similar or related functions are grouped together in systems. Eventually all the systems of a body come into focus. While still inside the mother's womb, skin, heart, muscle, lungs, kidneys and the brain all become defined. By producing the chemical messenger molecules unique to their cell type, these cells actually begin to take control over further development of the individual being.

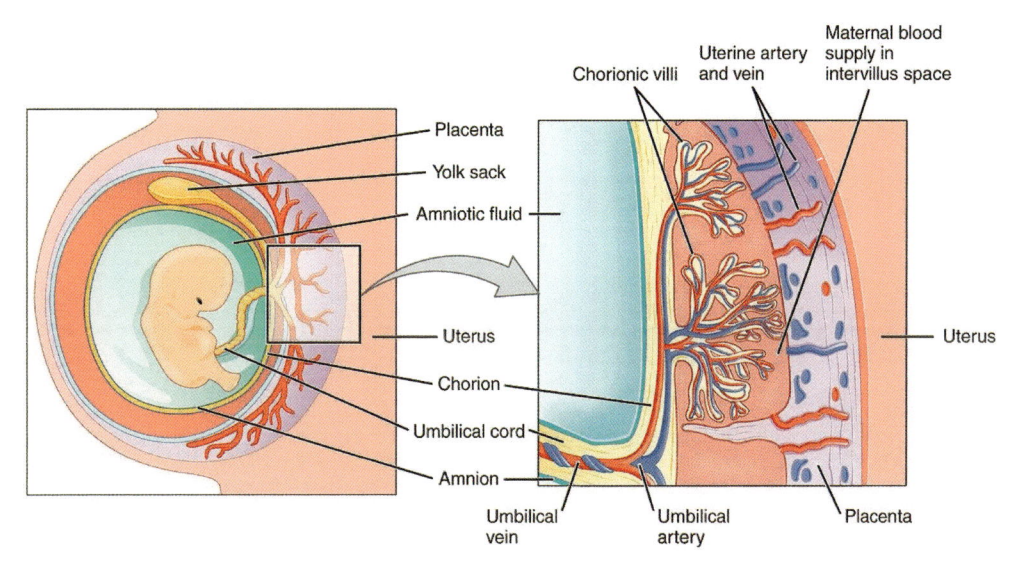

Schematic of the human embryo during gestation

Image courtesy of Anatomy & Physiology Connexions website via
www.commons.wikimedia.org/wiki/File:2910_The_Placenta-02.jpg

Anatomical and Physiological Systems

In humans, and other mammals, each body can be described as having these systems:

Circulatory
Digestive
Endocrine
Excretory
Immune
Integument
Muscular
Nervous
Reproductive
Respiratory
Skeletal

While these can be defined as self-contained structures, it is much better to think of them as functional units. Cells with similar function come together to form tissues, which then are grouped together into organs, but it is imperative to remember that all the functional parts are inter-related. Changes to one system can, and do, affect other parts.

The circulatory system contains the heart and all blood vessels, and circulates blood throughout the entire body. As the blood goes through the heart it receives fresh oxygen from the lungs, which is then distributed to every cell in the body. Along the way it collects carbon dioxide to return to the lungs for the respiratory system to exhale. Blood also delivers nutrients from the digestive system to all other parts of the body.

> Scientists have recently discovered that much of our digestive function comes, not only from our own digestive organs and their cells, but from our **microbiome**, an ecosystem of bacterial cells that thrive inside the human digestive tract. Our bodies are made up of many more bacterial cells than human cells, and they must be there for a reason! Possible functions of these cells may include digestion assistance, protection against more dangerous bacteria, and even regulation of our perceived feelings of hunger or satiety.

The digestive system contains the mouth, stomach, intestines and the anus, along with everything in between. Food enters through the mouth and immediately the body begins the process of turning food into fuel. Recall from the Chemistry section, that food is really just a whole lot of molecules stuck together! Some of them (like glucose) are usable by our body right away, while others need to be broken down into their component parts, or modified by various cells of the digestive system, before they can be used as fuel.

The endocrine system controls the release and absorption of all those chemical messengers that are so vital to the functioning of a body. It produces things as different as fear and anxiety, calmness and sexual desire, hunger and satiety, wakefulness and sleepiness, hormones to control growth itself, and even the ability to get tan instead of sunburned. Like the conductor of a great orchestra, the endocrine system directs the other systems to act appropriately and in concert with each other for optimal performance.

The excretory system is a lot less grand, but nevertheless, very important. (Imagine if we didn't have one!) The large intestine, colon, kidneys and bladder, and their associated organs efficiently remove waste products (feces and urine) from the body.

The skin also can be considered part of this system as it allows for moisture (sweat) to evaporate, thereby keeping the body's internal temperature within an appropriate range. The liver detoxifies anything that may have been introduced that is unhealthy. Bad fumes that we occasionally breathe or mildly toxic food that we occasionally ingest are rendered less harmful by the actions of liver cells. These cells have the ability to chemically modify the offensive molecules to either make them usable or get them excreted as soon as possible.

The immune system is in charge of our ability to fight off assaults of the biological kind. A body is assaulted every second of every day by myriad microscopic enemies. Bacteria, fungi, and viruses of all sorts attempt to enter our bodies, get inside their preferred types of cell, and then use our resources to create more of their own kind. Humans have developed a dual approach to defense. Some cells of the immune system are designed to act acutely, immediately fighting off anything that is not recognized as part of one's self as soon as the foreign presence is detected. This **innate defense** is common to every form of plant and animal life. The other type of defense is a more long term. Developed only in certain vertebrate animals, the **adaptive immune system** learns about invaders from the experiences of the innate immune system, and develops very specialized cells to attack these pathogens if ever a repeat invasion occurs. These cells produce antibodies that recognize the particular pathogen, enabling the cell to attack effectively whenever the pathogen is seen again. **Vaccines** are man-made versions of our adaptive immune system. By injecting a person with harmless bits of a dangerous (pathogenic) virus, we can stimulate the adaptive immune system to develop **antibodies** that are specialized to fight this pathogen. If we should ever encounter it in the future, our body will be ready and already equipped to fight.

Everyday Knowledge - Antibiotics

Antibiotics are molecules that are designed to kill bacteria.

They can act through a variety of mechanisms, which, in one way or another, disrupt the cellular processes inherent in certain bacterial cells. For example, penicillin works by damaging the bacterium's cell wall, causing the bacterial cell to essentially fall apart. The cell wall of most human pathogenic bacteria is very similar, and so penicillin is a **broad spectrum** antibiotic, meaning it can be effective against many different types of bacterial infections.

In any given population of bacteria, some will have a mutation that essentially strengthens their cell wall, and so they are resistant to the drug. Over the course of antibiotic treatment, as most of the "normal" bacteria are killed, the population can become enriched with these resistant mutants. That is why, if an infection is not eliminated with a first round of antibiotics, a second, often stronger drug with a different mechanism of action, may be prescribed.

Many antibiotics were derived from naturally occurring substances. Microorganisms (bacteria and also fungi) have evolved over the eons to compete with their ecosystem-mates, and this competition invariably meant weakening or killing their competitors. In other words, microorganisms produce and secrete antibiotics to kill other microorganisms. Over decades scientists have discovered many of these naturally occurring substances, purified them and isolated the most potent parts of the antibiotic molecules. Research often involves chemically modifying the natural substance in order to make it more selective in its targets or to lower toxicity to other cells. Other antibiotics have been designed from scratch by medicinal chemists to target a specific action of pathogenic bacteria. New antibiotic development is a very active area of research.

Everyday Knowledge – Vaccines

Vaccines are one of the greatest medical achievements of modern life. Consider all the human suffering throughout history - measles and mumps, whooping cough, polio. Consider also the horrible fate of people bitten by a rabid dog, before the invention of the rabies vaccine.

In 1998 one rather unscrupulous physician proposed a correlation between childhood vaccines and autism. Many parents were convinced by his statements, and a popular backlash against modern vaccinations was started. The fact is that this is an area of intense research, yet no other scientist was able to replicate the original "findings", and, in 2010 the original author publicly retracted his own work, admitting fraud. In other words, a complete lie was perpetrated on the public, with the result that today, after decades after essential eradication of these afflictions in developed countries, measles, mumps, and other childhood diseases are making a comeback.

Hundreds of children have fallen ill to these preventable diseases; several have died.

The **integumentary system** is what encloses our bodies, forming a layer of defense against all non-self entities, and keeping our own selves neatly tucked away inside. But our skin is not just a big bag filled with the rest of us. It is our largest single organ, and plays a very important role in numerous bodily functions. Defense against pathogens is certainly important, but skin also houses sweat glands, which keep our temperature fairly even, specialized cells called melanocytes, which protect us from ultraviolet radiation, and nerve cells which allow us to experience touch. Internal organs like the stomach and the lungs also are lined with cells (epithelial cells) which have similar characteristics to those of the skin.

> Every surface that you touch is covered with microorganisms and viruses, some of which may be hazardous to human health. The very first line of defense against these pathogens entering your body is provided by your skin in the form of DNA-ases, which are enzymes (protein molecules) specifically engineered to break apart DNA. Everyone's fingertips naturally produce these enzymes, as a first line of defense against whatever pathogens we may touch.

The muscular system, obviously, is composed of our muscles and ligaments and tendons without which we could not move. This, more than any other system, distinguishes animals from plants. **Skeletal muscle** is what we use in order to move around. Examples include the quadriceps (upper thigh) biceps (upper arm) and abdominals (yeah... those) which are controlled by the nervous system and move in response to what our brains tell them to do. In contrast, **smooth muscle** acts under the rule of the autonomic nervous system. The tension in our blood vessels, control of our bladder and inhalation and exhalation of our respiratory system are taken care of without much conscious control on our parts, yet they keep functioning day after day, and all through the night. **Cardiac muscle**, which makes up the heart, is a highly specialized type of smooth muscle.

The nervous system contains, most importantly, our brain and spinal cord (together called the central nervous system, CNS) and the myriad of tissues and cells called the peripheral nervous system, PNS. Some parts of the nervous system control voluntary functions while others take care of the business of staying alive, like regulating internal temperature and blood pressure, breathing, the processing of food into fuel, etc. Although the actions happen in different parts of the body, all is under the control of one or the other parts of the nervous system. Nerve cells (**neurons**) communicate with each other at synapses - teeny, tiny regions in which each nerve cell transmits or receives chemical messengers from the other cell. They also communicate with cells all over the body, as when a nerve impulse tells a muscle cell to flex.

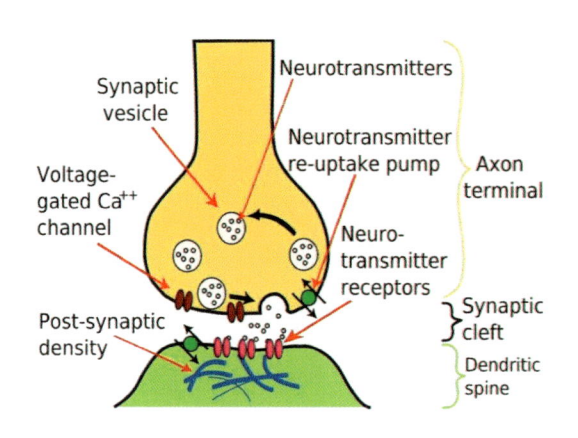

How cells communicate with each other

Image courtesy of Nrets, via www.commons.wikimedia.org/wiki/File:Synapse_Illustration2_tweaked.svg

The reproductive system governs reproduction, that is, the development of future offspring. From a species-survival point of view, the creation of future generations is the most important job any one individual has to play. Given that, very specialized structures have evolved to maximize the health and vitality of the sex cell producing organs. Comparative reproduction is fascinating, as many types of organisms have developed seemingly bizarre but elegant methods to develop their sex cells (a.k.a. germ cells) and get the sperm and egg to meet. How germ cells are created was discussed in the section on meiosis, and human development was also discussed above. While humans share the same basic reproductive strategies with most other mammals, there are some notable exceptions, like marsupials (the kangaroo) and monotremes (the platypus).

Other vertebrates, like reptiles and amphibians, birds and fish, generally use an egg-laying strategy for producing young. Some of these use a broadcast method, in which the females spew hundreds or thousands of eggs into the water, or other wet environment, and a male comes by and releases his sperm to fertilize the eggs. Then the parents are off on their way, leaving the (hopefully) fertilized eggs to the forces of nature. Others require contact between a male and female, so that the eggs are fertilized inside the mother's body. Of these, some mate with different partners each season, while others mate with the same partner for life.

The respiratory system provides for the exchange of gases from inside the body to the outside and vice versa. In humans and other mammals, the main workhorse of this system is the lungs, large sacks that fill with ambient air (relatively rich in oxygen (O_2) and expel what we cannot use, mainly carbon dioxide (CO_2). During inhalation, fresh air fills the lungs; it then diffuses into smaller and smaller branches called **alveoli**. The very thin walls of the alveoli are in direct contact with the equally thin walls of blood vessels surrounding the lungs, and, at that point of contact, oxygen in the alveoli is exchanged for carbon dioxide in the blood. The carbon dioxide now enters the lungs, rises through the upper respiratory tract, and is exhaled out into the world.

The skeletal system obviously serves as the foundation of our body's structure - it is made up of all the bones that form the shape of our trunk, arms, hands, legs, feet and head. There are 270 distinct bones in a human at birth although through childhood development some of these fuse together and an adult has only 206 bones. The skeleton is responsible for the obvious functions of support and movement, and protection of more delicate organs (as in the skull surrounding the brain, and the ribcage surrounding the lungs and heart). It is also responsible for the creation of all blood cells. The **marrow** of bone (the dark red, hard spongy stuff inside) is the site of all blood cell production in the human. Blood cells are produced inside the marrow, for delivery to the circulatory system. Bones themselves are made of an extremely strong composite material, which contains calcium, carbon, oxygen, phosphorous and also houses different cell types. **Osteoblasts** are cells that build new bone cells and **osteoclasts** are cells that destroy old bone cells to keep a constant renewal of bone going on. Bones also secrete a chemical messenger called osteocalcin which regulates how our body metabolizes sugar and deposits fat.

The take home message from this section is that all the systems of the body interact with each other in a myriad of intricate and complicated ways. Anything done to change one system invariably has effects in other systems as well.

Plants

Plants evolved on earth before animals, and the earliest ones were aquatic organisms - algae. Land plants evolved approximately 425 million years ago, during the Paleozoic era. The earliest plants were very small, low-growing types that by necessity clustered around shorelines. Eventually mosses, then ferns, came into being, followed by **gymnosperms**, the ancestors of today's conifers, and, finally, **angiosperms**, otherwise known as flowering plants.

Plants go through developmental changes just as amazing as those experienced by animals. Consider an acorn turning into a giant oak tree, or how the white fuzz of a single dandelion can spawn a field of yellow flowers.

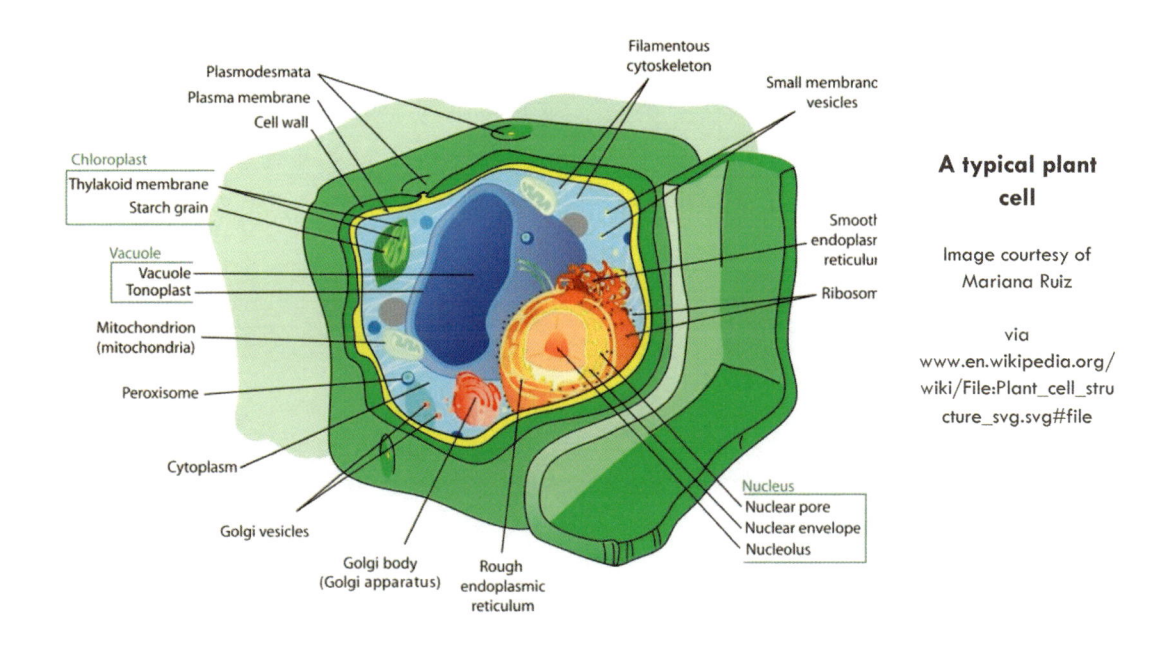

A typical plant cell

Image courtesy of Mariana Ruiz

via www.en.wikipedia.org/wiki/File:Plant_cell_structure_svg.svg#file

Plants are eukaryotes, and like animals their cells contain organelles which each perform various, specific functions. Many of the specific organelles in plant cells are the same as in animal cells, owing to our early common ancestors, but there are a few notable differences. Plants have a cell wall, which is much more rigid that the cell membrane of animal cells, and contributes to the rigidity of a plant's parts. Plant cells have a more angular shape, while animal cells, surrounded only by a relatively squishy (but very complex!) cell membrane, are rounder and more irregularly shaped. Plant cells have vacuoles, which hold the water necessary for a plant to live. This contained water also lends structure to the plant itself. Vacuoles also engulf waste products and expel them from the cell. Plants cells contain **chloroplasts**, and it is within chloroplasts that photosynthesis happens, as cells turn sunlight into oxygen and food. This is the single most important process in the world. Without photosynthesis, we, as humans, would cease to exist. All life on Earth depends either directly or indirectly on photosynthesis.

Some plants, like animals, have male and female versions, although some plant species contain male and female parts in a single structure. Male parts include a stamen, in which pollen is created, and the anther, on which the pollen is displayed for transport. Female structures include the pistil, on which pollen is received, and an ovary, which contains the female **gametophytes.**

In the same process of meiosis described above, sexually reproducing plants will create male haploid germ cells destined to pair up with female haploid germ cells to create a new cell with genetic material from both parents. In animals it's called fertilization. In plants the process of joining a female gametophyte and a male gametophyte is called **pollination.**

Pollination is essential for the propagation of a plant species, and so plants have evolved very specialized ways of getting their pollen to as many receptive pistils as possible. Some plants rely mainly on wind to transfer pollen grains to female plants; others rely on insects or birds to travel from flower to flower. As a bee, for example, sits on a pollen-containing flower, the pollen gets stuck to the bee. When the bee has consumed as much nectar as it can from this flower it travels to the next, and when it settles down onto a female flower, this pollen gets transferred to the pistil, where it can begin its descent into the ovary. The joining of the male gametophyte (pollen) with the female gametophyte results in a **seed** with genetic traits from both parents.

Close up of male (pollen containing) and female (pollen receiving) parts of a lily.

www.upload.wikimedia.org/wikipedia/commons/thumb/d/d5/Ritterstern_Bl%C3%BCte.jpg/682px-Ritterstern_Bl%C3%BCte.jpg

Evidence suggests that plants and their pollinators evolved concurrently, as changes in the shape of flowers provided an advantage for birds with certain beak shapes, or for insects with particular external coating, and feeding habits. Likewise, changes in a bird's or an insect's morphology could have provided an advantage for flowers with unusually shaped petals, or stickier pollen. Successful pairings of newer forms of plants and pollinators allowed for propagation of more and more of the newly shaped flowers, which in turn provided more and more food for that particular pollinator.

Bee collecting pollen

Image courtesy of Jon Sullivan via
www.en.wikipedia.org/wiki/File:Bees_Collecting_Pollen_cropped.jpg

Everyday Knowledge - Bees

No one likes to get stung by a bee, but bees are vitally important to humans!

Many bee species, but particularly honey bees, are necessary to pollinate food crops - tomatoes and turnips, coffee and cocoa, apples and almonds and many more are dependent upon bees for the creation of seeds to produce the next generation of plants. In the past few decades the presence of natural (wild) bees has fallen by approximately 50% across North America and Europe (actual declines are dependent on the particular region and time period studied). Termed Colony Collapse Disorder, this is a serious problem for farmers, who must increasingly rely on, and pay for, rented bee colonies for pollination. Pesticides, bee pathogens or parasites, or even unusual temperatures brought on by climate change are all under investigation as the possible culprits behind this devastation of wild bees. Perhaps CCD is caused by several factors. Whatever the reason, the loss of bees is a very real threat.

Classification

A very important part of elementary science involves students learning to classify things based on accepted lists of criteria. The fundamental system of classification of living things is listed below:

Domain
Kingdom
Phyla
Class
Order
Family
Genus
Species

Here are three examples of how this works for three organisms:

	A gray squirrel	**A Tulip Tree**	**Intestinal bacteria**
Domain	Eukarya	Eukarya	Prokarya
Kingdom	Animalia	Plantae	Eubacteria
Phylum	Chordata	Magnoliophyta	Proteobacteria
Class	Mammalia	Magnoliopsida	Gamma Proteobacteria
Order	Rodentia	Magnoliales	Enterobacteriales
Family	Sciuidae	Magnoliaceae	Enterobacteriaceae
Genus	Sciurus	Liriodendron	Escherichia
Species	Sciurus carolinensis	Liriodendron tulipifera	Escherichia coli

Until about the middle of the 20th century, scientists used simple anatomy (what an organism looked like) to assign plants and animals into groups that were as neat and tidy as possible. This classification system provides another good example to illustrate the changing nature of science. A brief history: In the mid-18th century, **Carl Linnaeus** came up with the first real scientific attempts to classify organisms. He was a brilliant man, and had some great ideas, but over time it became apparent that his system was missing quite a lot. He classified organisms simply based on the way that they looked, inside and outside. This classification system was revised and improved several times over the years, as scientists found new creatures or learned more details about those they thought they already knew.

In 1969 **Dr. Robert Whitaker**, devised the **five kingdom classification system** that was taught in schools through the 1970's and 1980's. But between 1969 and 1990, biological research saw an explosion of new ideas. Linnaeus' 300 year old system of classifying plants and animals is still fairly accurate in terms of classifying the things we *can* see, but the real cutting edge research is all at the biochemical / genetic level. Particularly, the study of molecular genetics proved that *on a genetic level* some organisms had a lot more in common with others than was previously thought, and less in common with some others that they had previously been connected with. (For example, the percentages of DNA that humans have in common with other primates discussed in a previous section was realized in the early 21st century.) Basically it was discovered that some organisms may look similar, but genetically are quite different, and others that look different may have a lot of DNA in common. We now know that the dinosaurs were genetically more closely related to modern day birds than to modern day lizards, even though they look more like the latter. This type of research is continuing today, and classifications will be revised if and when enough data show that a revision is necessary.

Dr. Carl Woese was instrumental in describing the most recent categories. Using genetic tests that could not have been imagined in earlier days, Dr. Woese came up with an extra category which grouped all life into three "**Domains**": **Archaea**, **Bacteria**, or **Eukarya**.

Archaea	Bacteria	Eukarya
Archaebacteria	Eubacteria	Protists
		Fungi
		Plants
		Animals

After the Domain, organisms are grouped into one of six "**Kingdoms**":

Notice that everything we can actually see is in the Domain Eukarya. All plants, animals, mushrooms and even some tiny, microscopic creatures are built out of eukaryotic cells. So why do the other organisms warrant not one but two additional domains? *What makes archaea and bacteria so important?*

First of all, look at the Tree of Life illustration and notice what a tiny fraction of life is occupied by animals. Human beings are just a tiny fraction of the animal kingdom. It is very humbling to realize what a small part of life we humans are. Except for plants and animals, some fungi (like mushrooms) and seaweed, *everything else exists in the microscopic world!* These are things that we cannot see.

Why should we care about such tiny things? Consider this: we are vastly outnumbered on Earth by these things that we cannot see. Microscopic organisms make up 50% of the biomass on Earth. The entire biomass is defined as the weight of every living thing — every microbe and every man, woman and child, every oak tree and every tomato plant, every dog and cat, every frog and every mosquito, and, well… you get it. Even more striking is that if you forget about land-based life and just look at life in the world's oceans, prokaryotes make up *90 percent* of the total biomass.

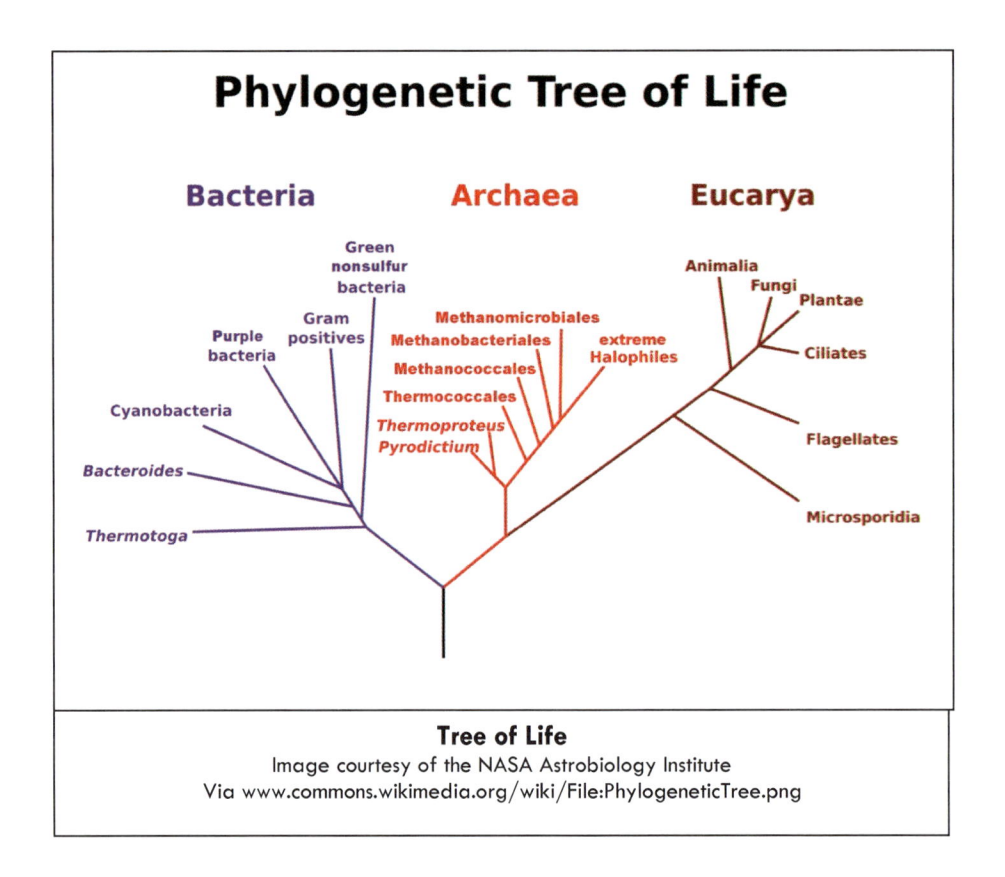

Phylogenetic Tree of Life

Bacteria — Purple bacteria, Cyanobacteria, Bacteroides, Thermotoga, Gram positives, Green nonsulfur bacteria

Archaea — Methanomicrobiales, Methanobacteriales, Methanococcales, Thermococcales, *Thermoproteus*, *Pyrodictium*, extreme Halophiles

Eucarya — Animalia, Fungi, Plantae, Ciliates, Flagellates, Microsporidia

Tree of Life
Image courtesy of the NASA Astrobiology Institute
Via www.commons.wikimedia.org/wiki/File:PhylogeneticTree.png

If that's not impressive enough, consider this:

There are more bacterial cells in the human body than there are "human" cells in the human body. In fact, your body contains about 10 times more bacterial cells than it does human cells!

These things we can't see can make us sick, but they also keep us alive. They are everywhere. They are in the air we breathe, in virtually every liquid on Earth, inside our bodies and on our skin. Microorganisms are responsible for nitrogen fixation, whereby they take nitrogen from the air and chemically change it into a form that can be used as a nutrient for plants, including most of the ones we eat. Microorganisms are used to make everything from food to medicine to fuel. Once we eat food, bacteria in our intestines allow us to digest it. Then, different bacteria living in sewage treatment plants or septic tanks further digest our waste. Bacteria are responsible for regulating the intricate chemical web that weaves throughout the entire Earth.

Microorganisms that live in the seas contribute mightily to chemical regulation of the oceans and atmosphere. Everyone has heard that trees "capture" CO_2 from the atmosphere and are therefore "good" for the planet and help reduce the effect of global warming. This is true, but what most people don't realize is that microorganisms that live in the oceans account for about 50% of CO_2 fixation across the entire Earth! When it comes to these tiny creatures, out of sight should not mean out of mind. They are incredibly vital components of the world we live in.

Kids (and adults too) should understand how all life on Earth is intertwined. Humans evolved on a planet brimming with microorganisms of all sorts. We can't live without them.

Everyday Knowledge - the Air We Breathe

It's easy to imagine a tree's leaves soaking up sunlight, but about half of the photosynthesis that happens on Earth (and, by extension, half of the oxygen produced on Earth) is done by algae in the oceans. Think about that - with every breath, you are taking in oxygen that was produced and expelled by tiny creatures floating around in the sea! Public discussions of the health of the oceans often focus on things we can see- like whales and coral reefs. But changes in the chemical composition of seawater can have profound effects on the microorganisms living there.

> ## *Everyday Activity – See What You Can't See*
>
> Buy a microscope! Scientific supply stores offer a variety of optical instruments that are inexpensive and easy to use. With a little hand held microscope you & your kids can explore your own skin and hair, leaves, pond water, puddles and soil for the existence of creatures that can't be seen by the un-aided eyes.
>
> To increase the magnification, visit a science center or museum. Many of these places have very high power microscopes set up for public viewing and will also have interesting specimens already fixed onto glass slides to check out.

THE FOOD WEB

When you are wondering where your kids get all their energy, the correct answer is actually, "from the sun". All living things get their energy, directly or indirectly, from the sun. Plants get it directly, and animals get it indirectly. There are three ways that living things can get their energy:

- by producing it;
- consuming another organism; or
- decomposing something else.

Producers are organisms that produce their own food. All they need is water and sunlight to make the sugars that become the plant's food. This process is called **photosynthesis**. "Photo" refers to light, "synthesis" means to make, and hence photosynthesis simply means "to make something from light". Photosynthesis takes place in a part of the plant cell called the **chloroplast**, which is a small bubble filled with a chemical called **chlorophyll**. This chemical has the ability, when irradiated with light, to turn water and carbon dioxide from the air into sugars. It's not magic, it's chemistry.

Consumers are animals that eat plants and other animals for energy. Small fish, black bears, mice, sparrows, zebras and vegans are all examples of animals who are **first level consumers**, getting all their food directly from plants that have made food from the sun. They are also known as **herbivores**. Many first level consumers become food for higher level consumers. Animals like wolves or lions are known as **carnivores**, because they consume other animals. Many animals, including humans, eat both producers and lower level consumers, and are known as **omnivores**.

Decomposers are all the things that feast upon what's left of producers and consumers after they die. Fungi, molds and some insects carry on this really important task. Decomposers have a strong "eeewww" factor, but they are really under-appreciated. What would happen to our world if they did not exist? Nothing would ever go away; dead things would just stay there. Poop would last forever. Decomposers do a lot of good for our planet (not to mention our back yards!) and should be given the respect that they deserve.

Dung beetles consume dung of all sorts

Photo courtesy of Rafael Brix via www.commons.wikimedia.org/wiki/File:Scarabaeus_laticollis_2.jpg

This brings us to the idea of the **food web**. For decades school children were taught about the "food chain", a concept which implies that there is a hierarchy to such things. This is a very simplistic view of things, and actually quite misleading. The relationship among members of any ecosystem is more like a web, with all creatures interconnected in such a way that disruptions in any one part of the system can actually have substantial effects elsewhere.

Here is an opportunity for teaching kids about human interactions with the environment. Chances are you may have heard that certain fish are not safe to eat at certain times because of mercury poisoning. Why do fish eat mercury? They don't actually want to, any more than we do. Certain factories used it in industrial

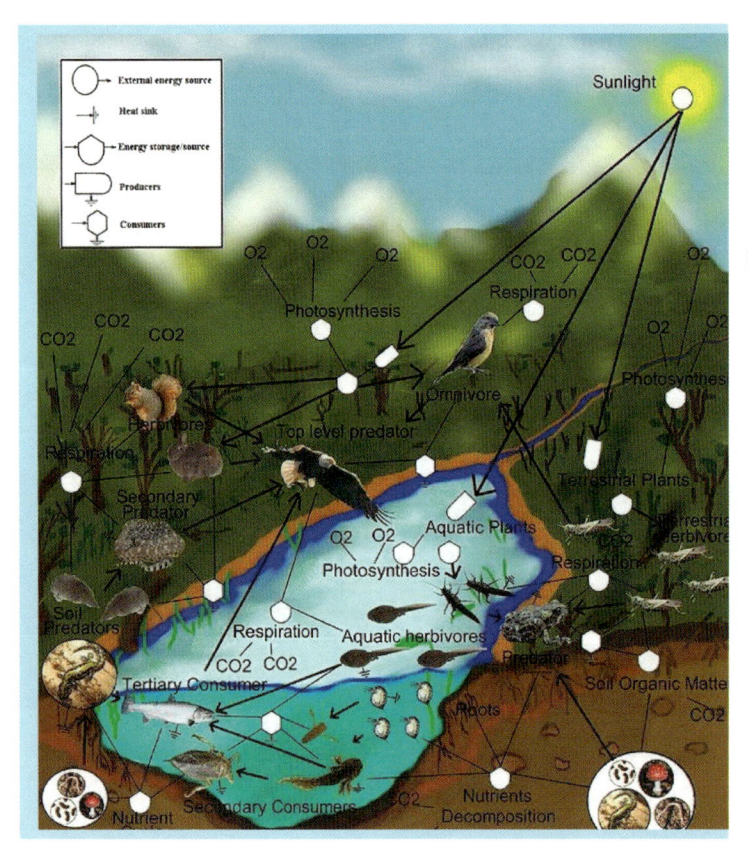

This Illustration of the Food Web shows how interdependent organisms are on each other.

Image courtesy of Mark David Thompson via www.commons.wikimedia.org/wiki/File:FoodWeb.jpg

processes and over time some mercury was released into the environment, sometimes deliberately and sometimes by accident. Once the mercury got into the water supply, it eventually ended up in the ocean. There it was absorbed by tiny shellfish and crustaceans. These were eaten by larger sea creatures, which were eaten by even larger ones. But here's the problem: *Mercury doesn't leave the body.* Once inside, it gets absorbed by the cells and stays there. A medium size fish may consume a certain amount of smaller fish in its life, but while most of its food gets digested and eliminated as waste, the mercury in its food gets absorbed into, and stays inside, the medium fish's body. A larger fish, such as a tuna, eats lots of medium sized fish and *all* of the mercury from all of these fish gets absorbed into the tuna's body. That's why, when humans eat tuna, we could get a relatively large dose of this mercury that was dumped out of some factory years ago! Not all tuna is contaminated with mercury. Tuna caught for human consumption is now tested for the presence of mercury and only tuna that passes inspection can be sold in the United States. But this serves as a good example of how interconnected we are with the world around us.

Revisiting the concept from the Chemistry sections, nothing ever really goes away. At the atomic level, all the elements that were here when the Earth was formed 4.5 billion years ago are still here today. Mercury that was dug out of the ground for use in some industrial process a hundred years ago, was purified, concentrated, used, dumped, and eventually flowed into the ocean. There it was eaten, absorbed into fishes' fatty tissue, and eaten again. When a large fish with mercury in its body dies, its remains sink to the bottom of the ocean, and the mercury goes with it. It eventually gets absorbed into new tiny shellfish and crustaceans and then into larger fish... **The actual atoms of mercury do not ever go away.**

The same can be said for any element. Chemical reactions change molecules (remember, molecules are atoms that are bonded together) and pluck atoms from one molecule and combine them with another. This creates an almost infinite array of different substances, but the *elements* never go away. Humans are very skillful at taking things from one part of the Earth and changing them or moving them somewhere else, but we cannot create or destroy elements. All the elements here on Earth, those in the seas, in the cells of trees, in the atmosphere, and in the cells of your own body have been here since the formation of our planet 4.5 billion years ago. They were born inside stars, and traveled across the expanse of space to reside here. They have become our planet and they have become us.

So … there you have it. Everything is connected! Neither matter nor energy can be created or destroyed, only changed from one form into another. From the earliest moments of our Universe, through the glorious cycle of star formation and supernova explosions, to the birth of our Earth, to the simple act of eating a tuna fish sandwich, the same basic rules apply.

Teach your kids about their world.

Watch a chemical reaction in your kitchen sink.

Pay attention to the weather.

Take them outdoors.

Look at the stars, follow the moon's phases.

Play with dirt.

Plant a seed and watch a plant grow.

Help them to see the amazing beauty, order and symmetry of Nature.

This is our home.

Help them understand how it all works.

APPENDIX - BASIC TERMS

The Metric System

Scientists everywhere, and everyone else in most of the world, use the metric system of measurement. It is easy to learn. The Metric system is based on multiples of 10. So 1 meter is equal to 10 decimeters. One decimeter is equal to 10 centimeters. There are 1000 meters in 1 kilometer. Unfortunately, aside from the standard "2 Liter" bottle of soda, or the "5K" road race, there are not too many metric measurements that the average American can relate to. Sure, you can easily get a computer to convert feet into meters. But it is helpful to get a real understanding of what these metric words mean and to have a mental image of what these quantities represent. Below is a list of approximations, meant to provide a mental image for the quantity, not an exact conversion.

Distance

Millimeter	• The diameter of a single grain of sand is about 1mm. • A grain of rice is about 3 mm wide by about 7 mm long • 1/32 inch – many tools and machined parts come in this size.
Centimeter	• A shelled peanut measures about 1.5 cm long and 0.5 cm wide.

	• 1 cm is about 2.5 inches.
Decimeter	• 10 cm is 1 decimeter, or about 25 inches. So imagine 1 decimeter as being very roughly equal to 1 foot.
Meter	• A mattress is about 2 meters long • 1m is about 3 feet, 3 inches long, or slightly longer than a yard. • In track races, the 100 yard course is slightly shorter than a 100 meter course (100 yards = 91.4 meters; 100 meters = 109 yards) • A meter is officially defined as the distance that a beam of light will travel in a vacuum in 1/299,792,458 second.
Kilometer	• 5K is a popular distance for running races, about 3.2 miles • Length of the Golden Gate Bridge is about 2.7 Km • The length of the state of Florida is about 720 kilometers, or about 450 miles.

Volume

Milliliter	• There are about 5 ml in 1 teaspoon; and 15 ml in 1 tablespoon • The volume of an egg is about 60 – 70ml • There are about 355ml in a can of soda
Liter	• Soda is typically sold in 1 L or 2 L bottles • A gallon of milk is 3.8 liters of milk • An Olympic swimming pool holds about 2.5 million liters of water

Mass

Gram	• A single grape has a mass of about 2 grams • A banana has a mass of about 120 grams • There are 454 grams in 1 pound
kilogram	• A newborn baby typically has a mass of about 3.5Kg • A large dog, like a German Shepherd, has a mass of about 38 Kg • A school bus (with no kids in it) has a mass of about 9,000 Kg

Exact conversions can be found at a number of websites. One of the best is

mynasadata.larc.nasa.gov/science-processes/the-metric-system

Exponents

Mathematicians developed exponents to make it easier to work with really big (or really small) numbers. Most kids don't learn about exponents until middle school but it is a very simple concept.

Any number squared is that number times itself, so $6^2 = 6 \times 6 = 36$, and $10^2 = 10 \times 10 = 100$. When you are figuring out the size of a carpet needed for a square room, you would measure each side of the room, say 12 feet, and square it: $12^2 = 144$, and so you need 144 square feet of carpet.

Any number cubed is that number times itself times itself, so $3^3 = 3 \times 3 \times 3 = 27$, and $10^3 = 10 \times 10 \times 10 = 1000$. The volume of a box (cube) that measures 2 feet by 2 feet by 2 feet is 2 feet^3 or 8 cubic feet.

In these examples, the ² and the ³ are the exponents of the main numbers.

Scientific Notation is shorthand using exponents. When describing things that are very large, like galaxies, or very small, like bacterial cells, scientific notation allows numbers to be written without using lots of zeros. For example, the distance of the Earth to the Sun is approximately 93,000,000 miles. In scientific notation this is written as 93×10^6. Exponents can be negative too, for example, 1×10^{-5} is 0.00001. A human red blood cell measures about 6 micrometers, or 6×10^{-6} meters in diameter, and the average adult human has 20-30 trillion, or about 25,000,000,000,000 or about 25×10^{13} red blood cells in their body at any given time.

Mathematicians and scientists also use the term "Orders of Magnitude" to describe things that are relatively larger or smaller by factors of about ten. This is a really simple concept with a very grand sounding name. To say, "a Labrador Retriever weighs an order of magnitude more than a Chihuahua" is mathematically correct. An average sized Labrador has a mass of about 35 Kg, while a typical Chihuahua has a mass of about 3.5 Kg.

> *Everyday Activity –*
> *Orders of Magnitude*
>
> Check out this classic 9 minute video of everyday objects compared and measured in terms of factors of 10.
>
> The Films of Charles & Ray Eames - The Powers of 10 (Vol. 1) (1968)

RECOMMENDED READING

Multidisciplinary Sources:

www.ucmp.berkeley.edu/education/teachers.php

www.earthscienceliteracy.org

www.nasa.gov

www.earthobservatory.nasa.gov

www.llnl.gov

www.loc.gov/rr/scitech/mysteries/

Physics & Energy:

www.physicsclassroom.com

www.school-for-champions.com

www.engineeringtoolbox.com

www.ucmp.berkeley.edu/education/dynamic/session5/sess5_electromagnetic.htm

www.coolcosmos.ipac.caltech.edu/cosmic_classroom/light_lessons/thermal/transfer.html

The Magic School Bus and the Electric Field Trip, by JoAnna Cole.

ISBN: 978-0590446839

Chemistry:

www.chemguide.co.uk/

Astronomy:

www.nasa.gov

www.earthobservatory.nasa.gov

www.llnl.gov

www.science.nasa.gov/

www.chandra.harvard.edu/

www.science.nasa.gov/astrophysics/focus-areas/how-do-stars-form-and-evolve/

www.particleadventure.org/

Geology:

Written In Stone; Raymo, C. & Raymo, M. Blackdome Press   ISBN 1-883789-27-3

Journey to the Center of the Earth; Harris, J., Gave, M., & Hincks, G.
Readers' Digest Children's Books   ISBN 1-57584-274-2

Rocks & Minerals; Symes, R.F.
A Dorling-Kindersley Eyewitness Book   ISBN 0-394-89621-1

The Granite Landscape; Wessels, T. & Cohen, B.
Countryman Press   ISBN 0-88150-528-5

www.maine.gov/dacf/mgs/explore/surficial/sites/jan14.pdf

www.thebritishgeographer.weebly.com/the-physical-characteristics-of-extreme-environments.html

www.eoearth.org/

www.education.usgs.gov

www.mnh.si.edu/earth.

Meteorology:

www.oceanservice.noaa.gov

www.whoi.edu

www.oceanexplorer.noaa.gov/facts/hurricanes.html

www.oceanexplorer.noaa.gov/facts/waves.html

www.oceanexplorer.noaa.gov/edu/curriculum/section3.pdf

www.ncdc.noaa.gov/oa/satellite/satelliteseye/educational/saffir.html

www.spaceplace.nasa.gov/en/kids/goes/hurricanes/

www.nasa.gov/worldbook/hurricane_worldbook.html

www.celebrating200years.noaa.gov/edufun/book/welcome.html#book

www.spc.noaa.gov/faq/tornado/ef-scale.html

Life sciences:

www.textbookofbacteriology.net

www.coml.org/projects/international-census-marine-microbes-icomm

www.BozemanScience.com

www.pbs.org/wgbh/nova/miracle/divi_flash.html

www.paleobiology.si.edu/geotime/main/htmlversion/archean3.html

www.geneed.nlm.nih.gov/

Acknowledgements:

I would like to thank all the generous artists, photographers and scientists who create and offer their works through Wikipedia under Creative Commons licensing. Without these resources, this book would not have been possible.

National agencies like NASA, NOAA, the U.S. Park Service and the U.S. Geologic Survey all offer websites that are treasure troves of information and inspiration. While they are openly available for all to use, in creating this book I have acted as curator, carefully selecting the material necessary to tell a story. I highly recommend taking advantage of all these organizations have to offer to the public in terms of information and education.

Made in the USA
Charleston, SC
03 February 2015